SMALLEST CIRCLES FIRST

Exploring Teacher Reconciliatory Praxis through Drama Education

Drawing from studies with pre- and in-service teachers in Quebec, *Smallest Circles First* looks at how teacher agency engages with the educational calls to action from Canada's Truth and Reconciliation Commission. Using drama education and theatre, *Smallest Circles First* explores how the classroom can be used as a liminal educational site to participate in reconciliatory praxis.

Smallest Circles First presents several arts-based educational research examples that illustrate how the arts provide a space for students, teachers, and communities to explore and learn about reconciliation praxis and responsibilities. By implementing arts-based counter-narratives set against settler Canadian history and geography, *Smallest Circles First* considers the implications of systemic racism, colonization, and political, social, and economic ramifications of governmental policies. Tangible examples from the book showcase how teachers and students can use the arts to learn specifically about their responsibilities in engaging with Canada's Truth and Reconciliation Commission, in addition to how this work can still meet curricular learning outcomes.

MINDY R. CARTER is an associate professor and the director of teacher education at McGill University.

Smallest Circles First

Exploring Teacher Reconciliatory Praxis through Drama Education

MINDY R. CARTER

UNIVERSITY OF TORONTO PRESS
Toronto Buffalo London

© University of Toronto Press 2022
Toronto Buffalo London
utorontopress.com
Printed and bound by CPI Group (UK) Ltd, Croydon, CR0 4YY

ISBN 978-1-4875-0549-3 (cloth)   ISBN 978-1-4875-3222-2 (EPUB)
ISBN 978-1-4875-2383-1 (paper)   ISBN 978-1-4875-3221-5 (PDF)

Library and Archives Canada Cataloguing in Publication

Title: Smallest circles first exploring teacher reconciliatory praxis through
    drama education / Mindy R. Carter.
Names: Carter, Mindy R., author.
Description: Includes bibliographical references and index.
Identifiers: Canadiana (print) 20210382058 | Canadiana (ebook)
    2021038218X | ISBN 9781487523831 (paper) | ISBN 9781487505493 (cloth) |
    ISBN 9781487532222 (EPUB) | ISBN 9781487532215 (PDF)
Subjects: LCSH: Drama in education – Québec (Province) – Montréal. |
    LCSH: Teaching, Freedom of – Québec (Province) – Montréal. |
    LCSH: Teacher participation in curriculum planning – Québec (Province) –
    Montréal. | LCSH: Truth and Reconciliation Commission of Canada.
Classification: LCC PN3171 .C37 2022 | DDC 371.39/9 – dc23

We wish to acknowledge the land on which the University of Toronto Press
operates. This land is the traditional territory of the Wendat, the Anishnaabeg,
the Haudenosaunee, the Métis, and the Mississaugas of the Credit First Nation.

This book has been published with the help of a grant from the Federation
for the Humanities and Social Sciences, through the Awards to Scholarly
Publications Program, using funds provided by the Social Sciences and
Humanities Research Council of Canada.

University of Toronto Press acknowledges the financial assistance to its
publishing program of the Canada Council for the Arts and the Ontario Arts
Council, an agency of the Government of Ontario.

Canada Council   Conseil des Arts
for the Arts   du Canada

ONTARIO ARTS COUNCIL
CONSEIL DES ARTS DE L'ONTARIO
an Ontario government agency
un organisme du gouvernement de l'Ontario

Funded by the   Financé par le
Government   gouvernement
of Canada   du Canada

This book is dedicated to all of the educators and learners who work on the edges, actively hoping, making, and creating places and spaces for social justice, peace, and love to transform prejudice, racism, and hate.

A percentage of the proceeds from this book, after costs incurred for its publication are covered, will be donated to the educational initiatives of the Orange Shirt Day Society, https://www.orangeshirtday.org/.

Contents

Foreword

Wat'kwanonwera:ton,
Ahniin,
Bonjour,
Greetings,

   Healing. Reconciliation. Trauma. Intergenerational effects. Resiliency. Residential schools. Indian day schools. All of these terms and more are in my vocabulary as a traditional support worker, a shako'tisnien:nens (a helper), working with my community members on the Kahnawake Mohawk reserve near Montreal, Quebec.

   In this time of COVID-19, the issues of grief, relationship problems, past traumas, generalized anxiety, and mental illness still continue and perhaps have been amplified by the pandemic. As essential workers, we hear and try to address health risks to our families, adapt to the isolation, address employment and financial worries for some, and deal with the uncertainty of how long we will continue this way. We have adapted as workers, moving away from face-to-face appointments with clients because of restrictions, to phone contacts primarily, but also making use of online applications.

   So, with this scene as the backdrop, it was a pleasant surprise to hear from "Mindy the Professor" about her request to write a foreword for this book. It was with honour that I accepted within minutes of receiving the offer, first because I could not find an excuse to politely decline, and second, because I felt confident I had something meaningful to say.

   Quite naturally, I recalled our first meeting during a KAIROS Blanket Exercise, where I was "Tom the Elder" working alongside "Lisa my friend," as we have done several times over the years. Clearly, Mindy as Settler had some theatre training and experience as the exercise unfolded for this group of students and then concluded with the talking circle.

The blanket exercise activity and talking circle involves something I love and feel passionate about: creating opportunities for dialogue, being honest and genuine, knowing ourselves a little better, and taking an ongoing learner approach.

A one-on-one appointment is similar to a group talking circle in that our aim in both cases is to create a safe place, a place where sharing of thoughts, emotions, questions, and learning can take place. The timeline of the exercise covers Indigenous people pre-contact, contact with Europeans, and the present-day context of Indigenous–non-Indigenous relationships. There seems to be a common theme among youth and adult participants alike. "We never learned this in school." "The events at the residential schools were terrible." Fill in the emotional blank. "I'm shocked, sad, mad, confused."

So, it would seem education on topics that Indigenous people face is necessary. The Truth and Reconciliation Commission's ninety-four Calls to Action offer a structured, concise way to do that. The *United Nations Declaration on the Rights of Indigenous Peoples* (UNDRIP) offers a legal framework for Canada to move the relationship forward for future generations.

Mindy the Professor provides evidence that drama and theatre is one way for teachers to introduce Indigenous topics within the classroom. And any person in formation cannot help but be changed and moulded by being a part of the educative, participative, and creative process.

It's a universal truth that we have a brain, and we also have a heart.

Lisa my friend is an administrator of a community centre and in training to be an ordained minister. She touches people by attending to both physical and spiritual needs. She also self-identifies as Indigenous of mixed heritage.

As a helper, I recognize that teaching life skills and educational pieces should also be accompanied by reaching the hearts of individuals. I include addressing spiritual matters in my trauma-informed work, and I describe it as our old Mohawk ways becoming new again. I recognize and applaud any work that is inspiring and healing and that highlights resiliency, caring, and compassion for everyone.

My time in isolation and closer collaboration with co-workers over Zoom has allowed an enhancement of cultural programs in which we have developed a Men's Support Group, an eight-week grief program, and an extensive healing program that will soon be ready to roll out. It has been my experience that clients can learn, share, and heal if the structure and guidance are there. Everyone has a story, and everyone is a historian of their own life, significant events, traumas, and successes.

And no one really knows another's story unless it is shared one-on-one or in a circle.

I want to tell you a story. Before 1990, I witnessed a local grade school play all about the interactions between Indigenous peoples and the Europeans as they came to Turtle Island. I viewed three productions of this piece since I was caretaker for the reception hall/stage that could seat 300 people. I distinctly remember my bosses complaining that the director and students were a nuisance and so demanding, and they couldn't wait until they were finished.

Besides parents and family, I was one of the few who enjoyed the production and the big, cute finale. Students had a time limit to assemble a puzzle of about forty cardboard boxes that when complete was a map of the Earth and its continents and oceans. The takeaway message: We are all Indigenous to Mother Earth.

Years later, Kevin, the director, actor, choir director, and my friend told me he appreciated what I did for the arts in the community. I was a volunteer for the Turtle Island Theatre for most of its twenty-year existence (now closed). I was part of an adult choir for nearly twenty years that did musical productions/variety shows in the spring and for the holiday season. Once the director left the province, the group disbanded, lost without its leader.

Now fast-forward from late 2018 to March 2019. A KAIROS Blanket Exercise was being held at a school for grades 5 and 6 in the West Island of Montreal, Quebec, and an invitation to collaborate and then view a play entitled *Reconciliation!* was sent by Mindy the Professor. It was like déja vu coming around full circle with the theme of reconciliation, moving beyond residential schools to exhibiting resiliency, and hope for future generations.

If one supports the arts, drama, and theatre, this can be a valuable tool to create spaces for dialogue and to unpack the stories around trauma of residential and day schools. It seems storytelling is a method to convey one's message and to generate discussion.

My day job as a traditional support counsellor involves allowing community members to tell their stories and offer cultural teachings, especially the Mohawk Creation Story, to make things right, to address trauma, and to provide a solid foundation for moving forward. My philosophy is that we are all lifelong learners.

My activities outside of work – such as collaborating on the play *Reconciliation!* discussed in this book – are also a form of education, of advocacy on behalf of Indigenous issues, and of promoting reconciliation and healing. One of the old teachings is to discern one's life purpose and then go about fulfilling it in one's lifetime.

Remember what the Oglala holy man Black Elk said: "The power of the World always works in circles, and everything tries to be round. The life of a man is a circle from childhood to childhood, and so it is in everything where power moves."

Come to think of it, I often work in productive circles: a Men's Group, a Grieving Group, talking circles, debriefing circles, restorative justice circles, the KAIROS Blanket Exercise closing circle.

One of the blessings of the pandemic is to have time for introspection. I realize that I have come full circle, from being impacted by two performances, at different ages of my life, to now wanting to have an impact on diverse audiences. I want to spread the message of the need for healing and getting along, the need to coexist in peace and live life to the fullest because this comes from the spiritual realm where Shonkwaia'tison "Our Creator" dwells.

A student eventually becomes like his teacher. An apprentice eventually becomes the master of his craft. A helper can become a healer. Through sadness, a person can become a lover, a warrior can become a peacemaker. A follower can also become a leader down an unknown trail.

Isn't life beautiful? Let these words and the content of this book act as seeds that produce creative ideas and beautiful actions in each of us.

Tom Dearhouse

SMALLEST CIRCLES FIRST

Chapter One

Starting with the Smallest Circles First

Two young women, both in their twenties, approach the drama education classroom at the start of the new term. Prior to entering, they take a short trek from the Faculty of Education building at a Canadian university, where all of their other classes are held, and enter an alternative place. This place is in a building which isn't on the regular list of classrooms for education students. It can be hard to locate, but once the young women find the correct building, they follow a colourful sign up a set of stairs and find themselves standing outside two big doors that lead into a large empty room with high ceilings, but none of the regular markers of a classroom, such as whiteboards, tables, chairs, or a teacher's desk/podium. Instead, they find a note that reads, "Please leave your shoes at the door." They giggle at each other nervously, take a deep breath together, and walk in. Once inside, they are asked to sit in a circle with their classmates and to prepare for an exercise their instructor calls "Coming to the Room," a phrase she learned from Susan Walsh, another arts-based educational researcher. Later, in silence, they lie down and are invited to focus on their inhalations and exhalations, eyes closed. As the leader of the class, I begin the meditation with these words:

Count to three as you inhale, eyes closed.
Count to three as you exhale and let the ideas of what you expect to happen next float away.
Give yourself permission to let go.
Repeat this process in your own time for three cycles of breath.

Slowly the nerves related to the first day of class, being in a drama course, and meeting new people begin to float away as they deepen their breathing and allow their muscles to relax. Now these young women who have just met for the first time, despite living and growing up mere kilometres from one another for the last twenty-odd years in and around Montreal, Quebec, Canada, lay side by side on adjoining yoga mats. In this moment, they have no idea what accepting the invitation "Come to the Room" may mean and how it will forever change their views of themselves, one another, their communities and classrooms, and even the perceptions they have held up to this point. As they later reflect on their experiences in the drama classroom:

> I went through all my elementary and high school in Quebec, Canada, and never learned anything substantial about Canadian Aboriginals. I discovered the issues Canadian Aboriginals face while backpacking in Australia and meeting Australian Aboriginals. (Arlene,[1] interview transcript, 2016)
>
> I found the activity that we did today (i.e., an improvisation on power) to be very eye opening in the sense that it offered me ideas of how I could approach Aboriginal issues in schools outside my community as well as my own. Often, as a Mohawk woman, I find myself sugar-coating the historical facts that I share on practicum so as not to offend anyone. I am an Aboriginal woman, and I don't want to hurt non-Aboriginals with the truth. But, now after seeing Shirin's experiences with hate crimes against Muslim women on the Montreal metro using Theatre of the Oppressed techniques, well, we all need to do our part to change things. (Teresa, interview transcript, 2016)

The tensions that Arlene and Teresa highlight in these quotes capture a part of the polarizing context that currently exists around Indigenous[2] content and topics in some Canadian classrooms. Arlene, a woman of European descent in her early twenties at the time of this research, grew up and attended all of her schooling in Quebec and felt that she "never learned anything substantial about Canadian Aboriginals" in schools. In the same province in her own community, Kahnawake, just kilometres away from where Arlene went to school, Teresa spoke about living as a Mohawk woman who was hesitant to "teach about Aboriginal people" when her cooperating teacher asked her to during practicum. And yet, after four years in their Bachelor of Education program, both young women chose to question their own knowing and not-knowing around Indigenous topics for the first time in the drama classroom. For Arlene,

---

1   Pseudonyms have been used for student participants as a part of the Research Ethics Board approval of this research. The names of other participants who are professionals in their fields (i.e., playwright, teachers) who have chosen to include their names in this research have not been given pseudonyms.

2   For a full discussion of terms used in this book, see the Glossary.

this impulse emerged as the drama class unfolded and she felt more comfortable in it. For Teresa, it was after a Muslim classmate came to school and re-enacted her experience of being harassed on a Montreal metro ride because she was wearing a hijab.

The experiences of these two students bring up a myriad of concerns that call for descriptions, definitions, and explanations in relation to the context of this research, including education in Quebec; curriculum and curriculum theorizing; Canada's Truth and Reconciliation Commission's (TRC) Calls to Action for Education; drama and theatre education; and teacher identity and agency. Each of these elements is a part of the research presented in this book. Each is an aspect of a circle within a circle, as understood through the teaching of "Start with the smallest circles first" in Richard Wagamese's *One Drum* (Lorraine, as cited in Wagamese, 2019 p. 80). Wagamese relates that "The smallest circles first" teaching was described to him when he threw rocks into a lake and was told that there are small circles that begin near the place the rock makes first contact with the water. From that point of contact, larger circles emerge and ripple away. In the drama and theatre education context, one also begins with the "smallest circle" of the self. This work begins as one centres the breath; connects with the body, mind and voice; takes off one's shoes; and chooses to step into an unfamiliar space/place of exploration, imagination, becoming, and belonging.

Teacher Agency, Canada's Truth and Reconciliation Commission, and the Quebec Arts Curriculum

It is useless for people to hear if they do not listen with their hearts ... and when hearts are open, ears can hear.

Chief Dan George, Tsleil-Waututh Nation, British Columbia, in his preface to the play *The Ecstasy of Rita Joe* by George Ryga

Drama ... is not life described but life imagined, it is possibility and not reproduction.

Howard Barker, *Arguments for a Theatre* (1997)

This is a book about elementary and post-secondary pre- and in-service teachers' agency in Montreal, Quebec. It looks at how this agency engages with the educational Calls to Action (#62 i and #63 i, ii, iii and iv) from Canada's TRC using drama education and theatre. It is about a quest that is hard to imagine given Canada's ongoing and historical colonial legacy. But, as Barker (1997) states above, "drama ... is not life described but life imagined." Imagining: to form a picture of something not actually present to the senses. One cannot quantify imagining when considering new ideas or counter-narratives, and indeed why would one want to? But one must begin "somewhere" and sometimes, as we have all experienced as a result of the global COVID-19 pandemic, we must adapt to change, cultivate resiliency, and grow in new ways, whether we are ready to or not. Between 2014 and 2019, I conducted two research projects with pre- and in-service teachers focusing on the question *What dispositions do pre- and in-service teachers need to develop in order to enact crit-ical-creative agency through the lived provincial arts curriculum?* to guide this initial imagining. This focus means that the content of this book may be particularly useful for settler or newcomer in- and pre-service teachers, or instructors of pre-service teachers, interested in learning about practical ways for using drama and theatre education to introduce Indigenous topics into classroom curricula.

Fostering Teacher Agency

To better understand teacher agency in Canada, de Britto (2018) offers a review of the interpretation of Canadian teachers' freedom of expression over the past thirty-five years. This review states that trust and professionalism are the purview of a responsible teacher, and that a balance between freedom and restraint is important when delivering the official curriculum. De Britto goes on to point out that there are "extended sites of control beyond school gates and hours due to [teachers'] professional identity" (p. 783). This suggests that teacher agency, or self-responsibility for one's knowledge, beliefs, judgments, and intersubjective identity (Phelan & Rüsselbæk Hansen, 2018; Edwards, 2015), cannot be separated from professional identity and freedom of expression.

Teaching in Canadian public schools means that there are reasonable limits related to what teachers can do and say in their classrooms when teaching the mandated curriculum and that teachers' professional identities often extend beyond school premises. While teachers clearly do have a right to voice their opinions, to influence and engage discussion, and to determine both means and ends with respect to their lessons, this right has reasonable limits established by normative social expectations. It follows that arguments for understanding and advancing teacher agency acknowledge the legal and social boundaries of the spaces that teachers work within, both on and off school grounds.

These limits are arguably reasonable for the teaching profession because they acknowledge the diversity of the Canadian population and the simultaneous need to function as a collective nation. However, there are contradictions within this notion that emerge on a "state apparatus level" (Foucault, 1980, p. 60) when one considers the effects of power/knowledge on an individual's body. For example, if the broad aim of fostering teacher agency through the arts curriculum is a viable proposition, given the parameters of the curriculum and teachers' willingness to engage in this undertaking, what are the limits involved in carrying out this curricular work? This question can only be fully considered in the context of the school as an anthropological machine (Agamben, 2004; Lewis & Kahn, 2010) where children learn

> to be quiet, stand in line, and place their finger over their mouths when in a hallway – or they will be punished by having privileges taken away, which also means no opportunities for experimentation through play. This machine demands a price from all young people. They become machines for the Educational Testing Services, future workers ready to play their part as money makers, and consumers patriotically saving the economy from recession, buying up anything just to rev up the engine we call an economy. (Snaza et al., 2014, p. 44)

To understand the impact of this state-driven machine and how power is enacted in relation to teacher agency, one only needs to zoom out from the specifics of this research and to return to a bigger picture of the realities that teachers in Canada face. At the start of 2020, in Alberta, the provincial government cut millions to education funding; Ontario teachers were on strike, asking for appropriate funding for special education, a strategy to address classroom violence, and fair hiring practices; and Quebec school boards were posed to be abolished and turned into service centres. Progressive arts education (as well as other departments) is weathering government-created storms, making the pedagogical, social, and logistical ramifications of enacting and operationalizing the curriculum for teachers challenging. The COVID-19 pandemic resulted in an exceptional opportunity to understand the relationship between schools as institutions and their provinces. In this time of global health crisis, the Quebec government enacted an emergency clause, which states that due to the COVID-19 crisis "the government is (able) to implement an array of measures to protect the health of the population" (https://www.quebec.ca/en/health/health-issues/a-z/2019-coronavirus/). This statement is reasonable given the situation that the pandemic created.

However, this public statement was a first communication from the provincial government to teachers across Quebec who had, at the time, been away from their classes for less than one week. This message further informed teachers and educational staff in the public system that their assignments, schedules, and workplaces could be modified at any time because their collective agreements were suspended. One could surmise that anyone would find this concerning and upsetting at any time. Since this information was sent during a pandemic, its impact was arguably worse. What we say matters as much as how we say it. The government's act of sending Quebec teachers and staff an email telling them their collective agreement is no longer binding raises the question: is it possible or realistic to foster teacher agency if the state can suspend a collective agreement without consultation or due process in an emergency? One wonders what the limits of teacher agency are.

Considering Bill 21[3] (2019) in Quebec and the ban it places on public employees' rights to wear religious symbols in the public sphere, we can see how teacher agency is paradoxical in the province. The circle of struggle and truth, a refusal or resistance to what the machine wants us to become, means that if teachers are "good" on the regime's terms, devoid of positionality, comply, and do not wear religious symbols at work (in this example), they can be viewed as successful in their jobs. However, as Hattam (2020) explains, when educators are effective at doing their jobs according to the rules and regulations of a system that is imposing restrictions that limit their rights and freedoms, there is no hope or possibility of agency because the rules of the system have already been internalized.

The Truth and Reconciliation Commission (TRC) in Canada

So, what is within the realm of possibility in regard to teacher agency, the arts, and social justice when curricular and legal limits are enacted? What is possible when seeking to integrate the TRC's (2015) educational Calls to Action (#62 i and #63 i, ii, iii and iv) into Canadian classrooms?

> 62. We call upon the federal, provincial, and territorial governments, in consultation and collaboration with Survivors, Aboriginal peoples, and educators, to:
> i. Make age-appropriate curriculum on residential schools, Treaties, and Aboriginal peoples' historical and contemporary contributions to Canada a mandatory education requirement for Kindergarten to Grade Twelve students.

---

3 In April 2021, the Quebec Superior Court ruled that Bill 21 would be upheld but that English-language schools would be exempt.

   ii. Provide the necessary funding to post-secondary institutions to educate teachers on how to integrate Indigenous knowledge and teaching methods into classrooms.

  iii. Provide the necessary funding to Aboriginal schools to utilize Indigenous knowledge and teaching methods in classrooms.

  iv. Establish senior-level positions in government at the assistant deputy minister level or higher dedicated to Aboriginal content in education.

63. We call upon the Council of Ministers of Education, Canada to maintain an annual commitment to Aboriginal education issues, including:

    i. Developing and implementing Kindergarten to Grade Twelve curriculum and learning resources on Aboriginal peoples in Canadian history, and the history and legacy of residential schools.

   ii. Sharing information and best practices on teaching curriculum related to residential schools and Aboriginal history.

  iii. Building student capacity for intercultural understanding, empathy, and mutual respect.

  iv. Identifying teacher-training needs relating to the above.

The TRC was officially launched in 2008 as part of the Indian Residential Schools Settlement Agreement (IRSSA). The TRC was intended to be a process that would guide Canadians through the difficult discovery of the facts behind the residential school system and was also meant to "lay the foundation for lasting reconciliation across Canada" (Moran, 2015). Over ten years later, the ways that the TRC's Calls to Action have been taken up are numerous and varied. Yet there is still lingering confusion about what the foundation "to be laid" is, what "lasting reconciliation" looks like, and how to achieve it. Books such as *A Knock on the Door: The Essential History of Residential School from the Truth and Reconciliation Commission* (2016) provide history around the legacy of Indian Residential Schools (IRS), helping to inform (often non-Indigenous) Canadians on the journey of reconciliation. In many ways, the increasing number of resources, such as this one, are helping to bring into the public consciousness this Canadian problem, one that former Senator and former Chief Commissioner of the Truth and Reconciliation Commission Murray Sinclair reminds us is a part of our shared history that all must learn about (CBC News, 2017). Sinclair, Ojibway, also reminds us that "[e]ducation is what got us into this mess – the use of education at least in terms of residential schools – but (that) education is the key to reconciliation" (Watters, 2015).

Reconciliation itself is a complicated and contested term or concept, as evidenced by some of the reconciliation projects throughout the world in Angola, Argentina, Australia, Bosnia, Burma, Cambodia,

Canada, Cyprus, East Timor, El Salvador, Fiji, Ghana, Guatemala, Haiti, India, Israel/Palestine, Ireland, Korea, Lebanon, New Zealand, Rwanda, South Africa, Spain, Somolia, and the United States. Though this list is not exhaustive, it is important to note that there is no way to universalize the understandings of "reconciliation" in these individual places, as each has their own historic and social context. In *Reconciliation and Pedagogy* (2012), Ahluwalia et al. bring together voices and conversations about what reconciliation as a term means and how this is a psycho-social and pedagogical intervention that aims to heal the effects of traumatic events: the spiralling guilt, anxiety, resentment, and senses of injustice that damage individual, national, and global well-being (p. xv).

Reconciliation means more than addressing the effects of colonization with Indigenous peoples in post-settler societies; instead, it can be understood in terms of a politics of recognition that involves an exploration of the effects of the relationships between memory, identity, and national identity (Ahluwalia et al., 2012, p. xv). This means that rather than defining reconciliation simply as the restoration of friendly relations or bringing something back together again, it is "not about the resolution or dissolving of differences; rather … it proposes a productive, hopeful space for imperfect, agnostic, and ongoing dialogue" (Ahluwalia et al., 2012, p. 2). As Tanya Talaga, an Anishinaabe Canadian journalist, suggests in her 2018 Massey lecture "All Our Relations," another way to think about reconciliation might be to begin by thinking about Indigenous rights and honouring existing treaties. For some, this may mean giving land back or recognizing self-determination while for others this may mean a substantial improvement in socio-economic, health, and education outcomes. Starblanket, Cree and Co-Chair of the North American Indigenous Peoples Caucus, takes this term to task by beginning with *The Oxford Dictionary*'s definition of "to reconcile":

> to "make acquiescent or contentedly submissive to (something disagreeable or unwelcome)." A synonym for reconciliation in the Oxford Thesaurus is "pacification." A synonym for "pacify" in the Webster's New Dictionary and Thesaurus is to "crush." The meaning of the word reconciliation is clarified … Reconciliation presupposes that past relations between the parties in conflict are conciliatory. "Re" means to do again and "conciliation" implies there were former peaceful relations. Is this the case? Has Canada ever been in peaceful relations with the Original Nations of Turtle Island? Peaceful coexistence requires one side not to be in domination over the other side. More importantly, peace requires truth … Nothing substantive has changed for Indigenous Nations and Peoples in this process. We remain colonized in a framework that destroys our national identities by the assimilation of

our lands and Treaty into the Canadian state. Reconciliation buttresses the assimilation project with words, policies, and laws that support the colonial project rather than dismantle it. (Starblanket, 2019, para. 5)

Starblanket's critique of the term "reconciliation" as a new process of assimilation that seeks to "re" pacify and subdue Indigenous Peoples is raised as a reminder that despite the conversations and work taking place in settler contexts, there are still serious concerns about the overarching narratives that these engagements are perpetuating and how the words used to re-story this particular assimilation project are not to be taken at face value. Along these lines, Madden (2019) contends that "perhaps in striving for clarity in both interpreting and applying reconciliation, it is not uncommon for knowledge about reconciliation to be asserted from a Eurocentric paradigm without acknowledgment of the ways in which such a taken-for-granted notion is anchored to Christianity and its particular modes, categories, and signs (e.g., dualism; civility and morality; reliance on confession, apology, forgiveness, and absolution)" (p. 289).

In the vast country of Canada, what is broken, how reconciliation might take place, and what rights need to be restored or granted for the first time are questions that cannot be answered once and then applied uniformly. This book does not aim to answer questions such as "what is reconciliation?" or "how can we 'do' reconciliation?" Rather, it presents several arts-based educational research (ABER) examples that illustrate how the arts provide a space for students, teachers, and communities to explore and learn about reconciliation praxis and responsibilities, which may be valuable to readers interested in taking up this work in their own contexts. Derrida (2002) spoke about a globalization of forgiveness that has been occurring since the Second World War, and while doing so made a distinction between forgiveness and reconciliation, and especially national reconciliation as a way to reconstitute national identity (p. 2). For Derrida, national reconciliation and what he wanted to call pure forgiveness, or an unconditional, gracious, infinite act, were both required in order for a "good" movement to take place. Thus, a challenge to shaping a collective vision of the future not only lies in the struggle for allowing diverse and sometimes discordant social imaginaries to coexist simultaneously but also to forgive or to continue to try when forgiveness feels too hard.

Truth, Responsibility, and Centring Collaboration

An openness to diverse and sometimes contradictory ideas is important because different people have different starting points when arriving at conversations about reconciliation. For participants from settler and newcomer backgrounds, broaching reconciliation cannot take place until they learn some historical truths that they have not learned prior. Dwayne Donald, Blackfoot scholar (2012), reminds us that often conversations about the TRC too quickly move to a focus on reconciliation, neglecting that there are multiple and sometimes contradictory truths that have been privileged in national and historical discourses. Settler and newcomer participants have to learn about residential schools; Indigenous loss of land, language, and culture; the implications of colonial governmental policies in the current Canadian context (i.e., missing and murdered Indigenous women and girls, Indigenous children in the foster care system, the higher than average instances of youth suicide, school dropouts, teenage pregnancy, birth rates, and the high levels of poverty for Indigenous Canadians); and how institutional racism plays a part in preventing changes from happening (Talaga, 2018). Teresa, a Mohawk woman and participant in this research, began by sharing her perspectives, identities, and lived experiences through arts-based engagements and encouraged others to focus on positive stories of resiliency. No matter where participants started their journeys, local Elders, community members, artists, and educators were there to share, teach, advise, and listen. Throughout the unfolding research process, James Charlton's (2000) "Nothing about us, without us" phrase, most recently adopted by people and groups seeking self-empowerment and self-determination, reminded participants of the importance of collaborating with Cree, Mi'kmaq, Inuit, Mohawk, and settler artists, educators, helpers, and Elders.

Specifically, Allan Vicaire, Mi'kmaq from Listuguj and the former director of the First Peoples' House at McGill University, led and facilitated all of the lessons for pre-service teachers in the first case study presented in this book. Allan further collaborated with students and the production team of *Sing the Brave Song: This Isn't Over!* in the second vignette/case study (2014–7). These research projects could not have taken place without him guiding the focus of the content presented to participants, or without his facilitation of the conversations and dialogues with pre-service students. Allan also introduced me to Ethel Stevenson, Muskego Cree and band member of Peguis First Nation, after one of our check-ins (in which we discussed how things were going with the pre-service teachers and how the creation of a play could evolve based on the research findings from the work with these participants). Shortly thereafter, Ethel worked with the playwright Alayna Kolodziechuk, a young woman of settler descent who wrote and directed *Sing the Brave Song*. Ethel offered feedback and thoughts during the development of the script and during rehearsals. In 2017, when Allan had limited time to continue closely collaborating, the opportunity to reach out and "expand the circle" of this research emerged.

Allan and I used the KAIROS Blanket Exercise with pre-service teachers. This is a Reader's Theatre activity that places participants in roles to learn about Canada's colonial history. I reached out to KAIROS in 2017 because I began a new research project with in-service teachers. KAIROS Canada is an organization that unofficially began working forty years ago and came together in an official capacity in 2001. It now includes ten churches and religious organizations that work together "for ecological justice and human rights." The KAIROS Blanket Exercise (see a sample of the script below) is "a unique, participatory history lesson – developed in collaboration with Indigenous Elders, knowledge keepers and educators – that fosters truth, understanding, respect, and reconciliation among Indigenous and non-indigenous peoples" (KAIROS Blanket Exercise Community, n.d.). In addition to being given cards to read, participants use blankets that represent the land in Canada and illustrate the effect of governmental policies and treaties on land rights during and following first contact. At the start of the activity, students place their blankets all over the room. A mosaic of overlapping colours, textures, and styles is the result. By the end of the exercise, the blankets are all lumped in the centre of the room, and the people who once walked freely around on any blanket they wanted to now find themselves crowded into a small space.

SAMPLE OF THE KAIROS SCRIPT FOR GRADES 4 TO 8[4]

Narrator: These blankets represent the northern part of Turtle Island, or what we now know as North America, before the arrival of Europeans. You represent the Indigenous peoples, the original peoples.

Long before the arrival of Europeans, Turtle Island was your home, and home to millions of people like you living in hundreds of nations. You fished and hunted and farmed. Each community had its own language, culture, traditions, laws and governments. These communities worked together and cooperated with one another. Before the newcomers arrived, you, the original peoples, ended fights by making treaties.

Optional: Consider having students form different groups and act out the tasks they would be performing on a daily basis.

Narrator: The land is very important to you. All of your needs – food, clothing, shelter, culture, your spirituality – are taken care of by the land – by the blankets. In return, you take very seriously your responsibility to take care of the land.

---

4 Retrieved from https://ied.sd61.bc.ca/wp-content/uploads/sites/112/2019/02/Blanket_Exercise_Standard_Edition.pdf.

Optional question: In what ways do you think that Indigenous peoples' needs were met by the land?

Introduce the volunteer(s) representing the European settlers.

Narrator: Things were happening in Europe at the end of the fifteenth century that would mean a huge change for you.

In 1493, the King and Queen of Spain asked Pope Alexander to make a statement that would help Spain's explorers when they arrived in new lands. The statement was called the "Doctrine of Discovery" and this is what it said:

European – Scroll A *(unrolls and reads in a loud voice)*: According to the Doctrine of Discovery, nations that are not Christian cannot own land. The Indigenous peoples living on this land will be put under the protection and supervision of the Christian nations that "discover" their lands.

After connecting with KAIROS, I was introduced to two Quebec-based facilitators of the Blanket Exercise: Lisa Byer and Tom Dearhouse. Lisa identifies as having Indigenous roots and is studying to be a United Church minister; and Tom is Mohawk and Ojibwe from Kanien'kehá:ka from Kahnawake Mohawk territory, and Anishinaabe from Garden River First Nation. Tom is a traditional support worker, or *shako'tisnien:nen*, who works on the Kahnawake Mohawk reserve near Montreal, Quebec. Together, Lisa, Tom, and I worked alongside Jennifer Hayden-Benn, an in-service settler music teacher in the West Island of Montreal, and her grade 5 and 6 students to create *Reconciliation!* This third case study centred on the relationship between reconciliation and collaboration, and Jennifer immediately reached out: to her administration, other teachers, and parents; to Barbara Diablo, Mohawk from Kahnawake, who taught the grade 6 students the Alligator Dance; and to Nina Segalowitz, Inuit throat singer from Fort Smith, Northwest Territories, who accompanied the students in two of their songs during the final performances. Jennifer reached out to the people she had ongoing relationships with, in order to help her students learn about content and culture during the play-creation process. Throughout the process of putting together *Reconciliation!* a continual loop of creation and feedback was established as various collaborators shared their thoughts with Jennifer and her students on everything from the costumes the actors wore to the images included in the set designs.

Relationality and Positionality

It is the strangeness of difference – the unfamiliar space of not knowing – that is so hard to tolerate for the colonizer whose benevolent imperialism assumes both herself or himself as the centre of knowing and that everything can be known. For the colonizer-settler engaged in critical inquiry there is an inevitable and disturbing moment when the Indigenous teacher or informant speaks. It is a moment of recognition – perhaps unconscious – that some things may be out of one's grasp. It is a fleeting, slippery glimpse of (the possibility of) something inaccessible and unknowable.

Jones and Jenkins, "Rethinking Collaboration" (2008, p. 478)

As the circle of people who worked on the various research projects presented in this book expanded from conceptualization to research, to analysis, and then to writing, debates around how to define, understand, and discuss reconciliation were front and centre. In fact, when Jennifer worked with Tom, Lisa, Nina, Barbara, and her grade 5 and 6 students on co-creating the school musical *Reconciliation!*, I was worried about calling the production by this name. I was fearful of entering the conversation on systemic racism and oppression too early, and fearful that I would lead with my feelings and opinions and would be "performing before transforming" while learning how to combat racism and become a better ally and ancestor (Justice, 2018; Saad, 2020). These fears stemmed from my own positionality as a white, cis-gender, able-bodied woman of settler descent because this work demands that I continually be in an "unsettled" (Regan, 2010) state.

In *Unsettling the Settler Within*, Regan (2010) quotes Sandy Grande, a Mayan American scholar who criticizes white feminist theorists who are "unwilling to examine their own complicity in the ongoing project of colonization … thereby ignoring the implications of power and privilege" (p. 24). As Regan goes on to say, non-Indigenous people have to situate and self-critique their own decolonization struggles. I take a cue from Regan in this respect and include personal narratives throughout this text as an "imperative to unsettle the setter within" (p.13). A part of this challenge is that, despite my many privileges, I grew up for a part of my childhood with a single mother who lived in subsidized housing, on welfare, in a semi-rural Canadian city (1988–94). I grew up for some time in a community where the realities of poverty – violence, a lack of access to higher education, and petty crime – were more common than family trips to the cottage, a fridge full of food, or a stable place to live. Prior to this period of my childhood, I attended Catholic schools and Presbyterian churches, where my father was the minister. The result of these experiences meant that it took me some time as a researcher and person to begin to understand how white privilege, religious indoctrination, white fragility, and institutional racism affect me. My awareness that I have been a product of colonialism came slowly because I was always worrying about working full time to pay for higher education, surviving, dealing

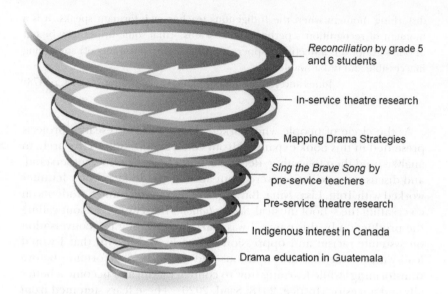

Image 1.1. Recursive researcher stance representing the years 2001 (Guatemala) to 2019 (*Reconciliation!*). Created by Graduate Research Assistant Alisan Funk and used with permission.

with my own lived traumas, and struggling for upward mobility rather than thinking about how intersectionality and marginalization work to stratify societal systems and keep dominant forms of power in control.

It wasn't until I volunteered as a teacher in Quetzaltenango, Guatemala, over twenty years ago and lived with a local family for a year that I questioned for the first time how I could be teaching the colonial canon as an English teacher to students there. I asked myself why I should be teaching what I had learned and how becoming "educated" in a particular way could change not only an individual's life but also the lives of their family. I thought about the effects of globalization on unique cultural identities and languages. These reflections made me think about my family, friends, and community in northwestern Ontario and about the conditions on Canadian reserves. This questioning led me to pursue my BEd, MA, and eventually PhD, with the belief that education and the arts can change lives or at least provide a seed for positive change, so that justice-oriented systemic change can happen.

The recursive researcher stance that began in Guatemala continues, and I still question what I am doing, how I am doing it, and how to be respectful and responsive to the communities and people I am working with.

At a particularly difficult moment of the writing process, I also struggled with using anti-oppressive and anti-discriminatory language. This led me to turn to academic and fictional books on my own and as a member of reading groups that were focused on reading and listening to more books, blogs, and podcasts created by Black, Indigenous, and People of Colour (BIPOC) (i.e., Blackstock, 2019; Cajete, 2006; Donald, 2012; Eddo-Lodge, 2017; Higgens & Maddens, 2019; Howard, 2018; Oluo, 2019; Saad, 2020; Talaga, 2018; Tuck & Yang, 2012). I also spoke about these challenges with Robert Hattam, a colleague from Adelaide, Australia, and with Tom Dearhouse, who both reminded me that by sitting with(in) these tensions we come to understand them, ourselves, and our work. To avoid the difficulties that arise, they told me, is to do a disservice to our research and larger communities. These conversations further reminded me of the relational ontologies that have been a significant part of my own connection with this work and how this research process is shared with collaborators, participants, communities, the land and the water where I grew up, and now, with readers.

Curriculum

Through its history, curriculum has become the way to denote what is learned at schools through content, pedagogy, schedule, organization, values, and evaluations (Funk, 2019). In this way, curriculum creates a system through which a society can reflect, understand, and enact its philosophical, political, and economic ideals. The value of viewing the curriculum in this way holds merit when the purpose of education and schooling is to maintain the institutional and societal structures in existence in a "particular way" for a "particular end." These institutional and societal structures have vested interests in maintaining certain content, structure, and control over what is taught, by whom, and to which students. For example, in English/Anglophone schools in Quebec, provincial tests at the end of the fifth grade are used to rank elementary students. Additional tests are administered in order to place these students in the province's competition-based high school system, where even public high schools starting at grade 7 have entrance exams that block access to specialized academic, music, technology, and sport programs. Such tests are just one way that prevailing approaches to education in North America, which are predicated on the belief that "the mind was ... a muscle to be exercised by memorization and recitation" (Pinar et al., 1995, p. 70), continue to reinforce a factory model of schooling from the turn of the twentieth century, so that students can be easily categorized and then trained for particular ends and means.

The classification of "Anglophone, Aboriginal, and Other Ethnic Groups" in the province's provincial educational and related documents are also reminiscent of Thorndike (1962), Bobbitt (1918), Sneddon (1921) – curriculum theorists interested in social efficiency. They and others saw education as a means of integrating minorities into a community where each level of "intelligence" worked at their appropriate level, and these minorities were socialized to accept it. Rather than integrating other cultures, schools were designed to teach minorities to fit in. In Quebec, where French is the sole official language, Bill 101 was established to alter the language of Quebec. Bill 101 requires, among other things, that children attend school in French, with the exception of those whose parents attended English school in Canada. A focus on community (achieved by conforming to the existing community) was the first focus of public education (Apple & Franklin, 1990) and schools served the function of creating labour stratification and socializing children for it.

Despite these deeply rooted systems and beliefs, contemporary curriculum theorists continue to rethink curricular approaches in order to provide space for transformative inquiry that allows teachers and students to develop agency, creativity, and imaginative approaches to content, themselves, and the world (Butler-Kisber, 2010; Carter, 2014a, 2016). The reconceptualization of the field began in the 1970s when Dwayne Huebner (1999) investigated phenomenology, Maxine Greene (1995) turned to imagination and creativity, William Pinar (1975) explored the autobiographical, and Philip Jackson investigated the hidden curriculum (Goodson, 1989). The dividing line created at this time continues to the present day (Funk, 2019), splitting curriculum studies into one half that unsuccessfully clings to the traditional, systematic form of curriculum development and evaluation, and the other, which attempts to understand curriculum (Pinar et al., 1995).

The significance of the process of reconceptualization that curriculum scholars and practitioners began in the 1970s can be mapped onto the research projects highlighted in this book, in which teachers are invited to use drama and theatre, a required subject, to teach about the TRC's educational Calls to Action, a topic not directly mandated in the provincial curriculum at the time this research began. This invitation is meant to offer educators the opportunity to express their own senses of agency, care, and social responsibility (Carpenter, 2019). Many curriculum theorists are also dedicated to dismantling systems of oppression (Apple, 1990; Giroux & Penna, 1979), or revealing other views of what can be known through artistic and aesthetic experience (Butler-Kisber, 2002; Carter, 2014b, 2014c; Eisner, 1979; Greene, 1995). This revision of the curriculum as an emergent, lived relationship seeks not only to teach the mind but also to nurture the soul and body in relational ways (Carter, 2014a), breaking the traditional ideas of what the curriculum is, and how it is created, taught, experienced, and assessed.

Contextualizing the Quebec Curricular Context

This focus on dismantling systems of oppression is useful for this research, situated in the Quebec context. Quebec is one of ten provinces and three territories in the country of Canada and is the second largest province. In Canada, which has a total area of 9.98 million square kilometres and a population of 37 million (Statistics Canada, 2018), each province and territory administers its own education, trying to meet its particular needs. Specifically affecting the educational decisions and demarcations within Quebec are issues related to the French language. French is one of Canada's two official languages, with English being the other. Long before English and French were the colonial and now "official" languages spoken in the province, Mohawk, Ojibwe, and Cree were (and are still) spoken (Cook & Flynn, as cited in Archibald, 2008). The ten "Quebec" First Nations include the Abenaki, Algonquin, Atikamekw, Cree, Malecite, Huron-Wendat, Innu, Mi'kmaq, Mohawk, and Naskapi.

The Quebec Education Plan (QEP; Ministère de l'Éducation et de l'Enseignement supérieur [MEES], 2016) is a provincially mandated curricular document that outlines the requirements for both English and French K–11 education in the province. There are separate French and English documents of the QEP. In Quebec, the public system consists of sixty-nine school boards, sixty of which are French-language school boards and nine are English-language school boards. In addition, there are three special-status school boards (Littoral, Kativik, and Cree) and the Naskapi School. The private school system consists of 290 institutions: 187 of these are accredited to receive Quebec government grants, and the other 103 are certified but do not receive these grants.

In Quebec, there is also an underrepresentation of "visible minority" (VM) teachers.[5] In 2006, the number of teachers in Quebec was 101,365, and the number of VM teachers was 3,985 or 3.9 per cent (Ryan et al., 2009, p. 598). Since "racial origins influence teachers' perceptions and … lived experiences influence teachers' views" (Carr & Klassen, 1997, p. 77), who the teachers are – culturally, racially, linguistically, religiously – matters. Given the substantially lower number of VM teachers in Quebec,

---

5 Despite the United Nations drawing attention to the discriminatory nature of the term "visible minority" within Canada's Employment Equity Act, where visible minorities are defined as persons other than Aboriginal people, who are non-Caucasian in race or non-white in colour, this term is still used.

one must consider what narratives are being told and retold, simply because certain individuals, with their own particular subjectivities, make up the majority of the teachers in the province.[6]

Language, Culture, and Religion in Quebec Education[7]

Though this book is not focused on discussing a comprehensive history of education in Quebec, it is important to provide context regarding the significance of language, culture, and religion in the province given the impact of governmental policies on the province's educational system. In fact, the first school in Quebec has been traced to the arrival of the Recollect missionaries who arrived in Quebec City in the early 1600s. Samuel de Champlain brought them from France with the hope that a spiritual ministry would flourish in New France, resulting in the Recollects (Catholic friars and nuns) becoming the first elementary school teachers in the province. As Charbonneau (2018) discusses, the system of political thought rooted in Catholic doctrine, specifically called *Rerum Novarum* (1890) and *Quadragesimo Anno* (1931), continued to inform all aspects of institutional thought until the twentieth century. Following this religious history related to schooling, the provincial school boards were designated as the "Protestant School Board" and the "Catholic School Board" until the Quiet Revolution in the 1960s. This meant that students from Protestant backgrounds would go to Protestant schools and students from Catholic backgrounds would go to Catholic schools. The Quiet Revolution, centred on the need for a new theory of federalism and political economy that focused on secularization and sovereignty, caused ripple effects across all socio-cultural and political systems in the province.

Part of the ramifications of this political and cultural shift was a change to the educational system in Quebec, in which a division between French

---

6 The *Rapport Triennal* (2016–19), a 127-page report released by the Quebec Human Right's Commission, stated that there is a lack of progress in bringing VM into the public service. As of 2019, Quebec's representation of VM in civil service was 6.3 per cent while the national average was 10.3 per cent. Based on the percentage of VM in Quebec, 13 per cent of civil servants should be VM.

7 As an English speaker who studied French in Canadian public schools (K–OAC in Manitoba and Ontario) I still do not have a strong enough grasp of the language to read and comprehend provincial and academic texts in French. For this reason, I have only read available English documents on education in Quebec. There are some Quebec educational documents that are only available in French and there is additional literature by French scholars on education that has not been translated. For these reasons, the research and discussions represented in this book do not include an analysis of French educational documents, which sometimes have additional details that are not in the English translations. This has affected my perspectives.

and English emerged in order to guarantee the linguistic and cultural maintenance and development of each group. "Other than making the knowledge of French an important asset for upward economic mobility, the adoption of the Charter of the French Language in 1977 (Bill 101) further made French language schooling the norm for an overwhelming majority of French-speaking and immigrant students" (Zanazanian, 2008, p. 112). Part of the educational impact of Bill 101 was an increase in the number of school-aged students attending private schools in the province, since the schools were given the option of opting out of government funding in return for linguistic and cultural autonomy. Effectively, this separated schools along cultural and language lines, placing children and youth into a variety of private schools – Greek, Armenian, Catholic, English, Jewish, and so on – many of which do not receive government subsidies.

The educational implications of these political shifts have not only led to an increase in private school enrolment across the province but also to an increase in tensions between proponents of the transmission of the Franco-Québécois collective identity and those interested in producing critically engaged citizens that are fundamentally open to minority viewpoints (Cardin, 2004; Lévesque, 2004; B. Young, 2006). This has profoundly impacted the Allophone community (those whose first language is not English or French) in the province, because they have been required to send their children to French school.

The Education of "Anglophone, Aboriginal, and Groups of Other Ethnic Origins"

When the Quebec-centred nationalist curriculum was first proposed, the Quebec Ministry of Education's 1998 Policy Statement on Educational Integration and Intercultural Education spoke to the public's concern, proposing to "integrate into the study of history – not just to tack on as separate material – the role played by Anglophones and Aboriginal peoples, and by groups of other ethnic origins, in the building of Québec society and development of the collective identity and memory of Québecers" (Ministère de l'Éducation, 1998, p. 26). This is significant not only because the statement indicates that the histories of "Anglophones, Aboriginals, and People with Other Ethnic Origins" must be integrated into the study of Quebec history (because they are currently merely "tacked on") but because they are all grouped together as a list of "others."

Offering an alternative to the single narrative of what it means to be a "Quebecer," the 2003 curriculum reform in the province shifted its focus to include a "collective identity narrative reference framework ... that is more accessible to social diversity within a socio-constructivist mind frame

[by giving a more] prominent role [to] questioning and interpreting social realities" (Ministère de l'Éducation, du Loisir et du Sport [MELS],
2003). On paper, this shift towards a collective identity that is more accessible to social diversity using interpretation and questioning sounds like
a positive change. However, the political will to support these shifts for
greater diversity was called into question by the widespread support for
Bill 21 (The Canadian Press, 2019). For educators and pre-service teachers, this sends a strong message that certain individuals are not welcome
in public schools because of their religious and cultural practices.

Other provincial mandates that affect the QEP and education practices
in the province include the Charter of the French Language (Bill 101),
and Bill 115, An Act Following Upon the Court Decisions on the Language of Instruction. Bill 115, passed in 2010, amends the Charter of the
French Language and states that all children must be educated in French
until the end of their secondary studies, whether in a public school or a
subsidized private school. Thus, despite an official curricular stance to include more diverse perspectives within the Quebec curriculum, there was,
and still is, a great division between Francophone and "Other" realities
that continues to directly impact the educational systems in the province.
Linda Handiak, a private school history teacher in Montreal, contends
that this also means that "Indigenous experiences, history and culture in
Quebec are taught in relation to the colonization of Canada with a dominant French narrative, if they are taught at all" (L. Handiak, personal communication, November 15, 2018). As evidenced by Arlene's experiences,
omitting histories that do not prioritize those of the Franco-Quebecers, or
situating them solely in relation to this Franco-dominant narrative, means
that decades of students in K–11 may not have learned "anything significant" about Indigenous peoples (Arlene, interview transcript, 2016). This
is also the curricular context of the research for this book.

Are the Arts the Answer?

There is a crack, a crack in everything/That's how the light gets in.
                              Leonard Cohen, "Anthem" (1992)

As described at the start of this chapter, teacher agency has to be
contextualized within the institutional and societal framework teachers
live and work in. While teachers may have some agency in the ways that
they teach their subjects, there are still curricular outcomes to meet and
standardized tests to prepare for. Specifically in Quebec, teacher agency
has been further impacted by governmental legislation. This might seem

as though a teacher's capacity to act independently and to make their own free choices are antithetical to the Quebec context.

However, within the arts education curriculum for K–11 in Quebec, there is an opening for the inclusion of reconciliation pedagogies or other meta-narratives to be legitimately created (MEES, 2001). In the Quebec Education Program, chapter 8 is dedicated to arts education. Within this chapter, the overarching goal of arts education (i.e., drama, dance, music, and visual art) is for "these subjects [to] enable students to express their own reality and vision of the world and [to] help them to communicate their inner images through the creation and interpretation of artistic productions" (MEES, 2001, p. 206). Furthermore, the core learning outcomes for art education are for students to be able to achieve the following:

- Communicate and give concrete expression to [their] ideas, inner images, impressions, sensations and emotions in various artistic productions, by using or considering elements and principles specific to the artistic languages used; and
- Appreciate facets of his/her own works and those of classmates, as well as works by men and women of the past and present, from here and elsewhere, by referring to varied criteria and expressing himself/herself orally or in writing. (MEES, 2001, p. 207)

This means that the arts education curriculum in the province of Quebec has the space for meta-narratives related to learning, representing, and communicating about "men and women of the past and present, from here and elsewhere." As a high school teacher in Quebec from 2007 to 2009, I received training in the current QEP. A part of this training was on the importance of cross-curricular integration versus subject-related silos. Practically speaking, this meant that I was encouraged to create integrated projects with other subject area teachers so students could learn about key information in transdisciplinary ways. Beyond the general outcomes of the arts education curriculum in the QEP, section 8.1 focuses on the outcomes of drama education:

- Drama involves the creation and interpretation of works in which characters interact. Through different forms of creation, expression and communication, the subject allows students to represent inner images in different ways and in various contexts. It also allows for the expression of a sociocultural reality. Furthermore, drama offers the opportunity to portray stories and characters in action using elements of a stage

set in front of an audience and following certain conventions which
may vary according to place and historical period.

- Drama education, in the context of continuous progress throughout
  elementary school, develops the students' artistic sensibility, creative
  potential, acting abilities and skills in self-expression and communication. Through a variety of affective, cognitive, psychomotor, social and
  aesthetic experiences, students have an opportunity to express their
  ideas, personal vision of the world, those of their classmates and those
  of playwrights or other creators.
- Throughout their drama education in elementary school, students are
  introduced to numerous references from their immediate cultural environment or related to the works they are interpreting and appreciating.
  They are also encouraged to make connections with cultural references
  in other subjects. In so doing they acquire an openness to the world,
  discover its particular features and differences, and gain a better understanding of their own culture. This renewed and enriched view of the
  world helps students to develop their own cultural identity and prepares
  them for their role as citizens.
- To invent their own short scenes, students engage in a creative process
  and make use of different stimuli for creation and the many possibilities
  of dramatic language, performance techniques, styles of theatre and
  elements of drama. In interpreting a variety of short scenes, they will
  broaden their general knowledge of culture through direct contact with
  dramatic works. (MEES, 2001, p. 212)

As illustrated above, the main criteria for drama education in the QEP
is to ensure that students are able to use their bodies, minds, creativity,
and aesthetic sensibilities to make sense of themselves, their worlds, different cultures, and others in various historical periods using the techniques of drama within a classroom or theatre performance space. This
is all done in order for students to get a better understanding of who
they and others are, and to acquire an openness to the world. The rest of
the drama education criteria goes on to describe particular techniques
(i.e., Reader's Theatre, improvisation, movement) that can be used to
support these objectives.

Vignettes

The three case studies or vignettes in this book were selected as exemplars for how primarily pre- and in-service teachers in Quebec use teacher
agency to engage with the TRC's educational Calls to Action while creating
collaborative drama and theatre performances. For readers interested in

taking up the Calls to Action in the TRC, these vignettes cover a range of practical pre- and in-service K-University contexts using both drama education and theatre performances to learn and present shared understandings. The diverse examples of how students and teachers can use the arts to take up the TRC's Calls to Action in pedagogical spaces are a reminder that there is no formula that can be applied in all instances. This is the case because the unique collaborative communities that develop in the rehearsal space are contingent upon the individuals who contribute to the conversations, learning, and community. Data for the vignettes come from two research projects, one funded by the Social Sciences and Humanities Research Council (SSHRC): *Mapping Drama and Theatre Strategies and the Impact of Play Building with In-service Teachers* (2018–20) and one by the Fonds de Recherche du Québec – Société et Culture (FRQSC): *The Pre-Service Teacher Monologues: Exploring Indigenous Topics through Drama and Theatre Education in Québec* (2015–17). Table 1.1 provides a broad overview of the case studies embedded within these two research grants. The overarching research question for this book is used across all three case studies: What dispositions do pre- and in-service teachers need to develop in order to enact critical-creative agency through the lived provincial arts curriculum?

Vignette 1: The Pre-Service Teacher Monologues (2015–16)

As shown in Table 1.1, each vignette has unique data sources and a variety of forms of data. In *The Pre-Service Teacher Monologues*, the participants include five BEd students: Heidi, Astrid, Max, Arlene, and Teresa. Their participation entailed taking part in the curriculum and instruction in drama education class and keeping a journal of their experiences. Participants were recruited from my drama class by a Research Assistant (RA) on the second day of classes. As soon as I was finished teaching, the RA came in, described the opportunity to be a part of the project, and explained that all correspondence about the research project had to go through her until I submitted grades for the regular drama class – this was stipulated as a part of McGill University's ethics approval because I would be their instructor and research lead. Max and Heidi elected to participate in the fall term and Astrid, Arlene, and Teresa in the winter term.

The regular outcomes for the class were maintained for the course; however, there was a special focus on the TRC weaved throughout, which Allan Vicaire helped to create and teach. Topics included residential schools, systemic oppression and racism, the Sixties Scoop, colonial practices in Canada and their long-term implications, treaties in Canada, the division of land and creation of reserves in Canada, missing and murdered Indigenous women and girls, poverty, and lack of access to basic

Table 1.1. Overview of Individual Vignettes

Case study/ vignette	Participants	Research Site	Study-specific Research Question	Timeline	Sources of Data Collected	Forms of Analysis	Sample of Emergent Themes
The Pre-Service Teacher Monologues	5 BEd students in Curriculum and Instruction in Drama Education Allan Vicaire, Mi'kmaq	Classroom space at McGill University (Montreal, QC)	What are your lived experiences co-creating a monologue on an issue of personal significance?	2015–16	Writing Monologues Journals Participant Observation Theatre creation Interviews and focus groups Photos	Constant comparison using narrative analysis to code for descriptive and then conceptual themes	Healing Art for advocacy Embodiment and Appropriation Racism
Sing the Brave Song: This Isn't Over!	4 actors Alayna Kolodziechuk, Playwright Stage manager/RA Ethel Stevenson, Cree Elder Audience members Invited panel	Rehearsal space and Theatre on McGill campus (Montreal, QC)	How can theatre and arts-based educational research help to educate and foster critical conversations about the TRC?	2017	Script Focus group interviews Observation of rehearsals and performances Audience surveys Invited panel conversations Feedback from Ethel on script Photos	Constant comparison using narrative analysis to code for descriptive and then conceptual themes	White fragility and Racism Being in Solidarity and Becoming an Ally Learning through the arts to develop pedagogical competency Appropriation
Reconciliation!	Jennifer Hayden-Benn Tom Dearhouse, Mohawk Elder Barbara Diablo, Mohawk artist Lisa Byer (KAIROS)	Elementary School (Beaconsfield, QC)	What are the experiences of an in-service Quebec teacher using theatre to create an original production?	2018–19	Interviews Observations Photos Original script and songs Media coverage	NVivo to code for descriptive themes and constant comparison to develop conceptual themes	Relationships and community support Teacher agency

Note: The forms of analysis particular to each vignette and the subsequent emergent themes from each individual study are illustrated in this table to represent the large and detailed data sets that were analysed as a part of the research in this book. The specific data, analysis and research questions related to each vignette/case study are not described in detail in order to ensure that a more uniform narrative was told about the experiences of in- and pre-service teachers in Quebec using the arts to explore and teach the TRC's Calls to Action for Education. I've chosen instead to use cross-cutting themes and the overarching research question to present this research.

Image 1.2. Allan Vicaire leading a conversation with students at the completion of the KAIROS Blanket Exercise with the Fall 2015 drama class. Photo by Layal Shuman, Research Assistant.

rights on reserves. Students were then asked to create a final performance piece on their inquiry of an issue. The students' written journals about the creation of their performance and in-class responses about their final monologues were collected and post-course interviews took place.

Vignette 2: Sing the Brave Song: This Isn't Over! (2017)

Participants in the second vignette included four actors, a stage manager, and Alayna Kolodziechuk, the playwright/director who wrote the theatre piece that explored the TRC. Allan Vicaire and Ethel Stevenson shared their thoughts on the script throughout the development and rehearsal process, leading the actors and director/playwright to rewrite, rehash, research, and restate their thoughts, experiences, and perspectives on reconciliation and what the TRC's Calls to Action meant to them as settlers.

Image 1.3. Actors in *Sing the Brave Song* rehearsing a scene about the challenges of incorporating content in response to the TRC into the Quebec curriculum (see appendix 1 for full script). Photo taken by the author.

Prior to the performance of *Sing the Brave Song: This Isn't Over!* on 18 and 19 May 2017, rehearsals took place three times a week from mid-February to mid-May 2017. In addition to the content of the play being presented through performance, a videographer was hired to put together a series of images and clips that the playwright wished to include using open-access materials. After each performance, audience members were invited to provide written feedback about their impressions of the play. Twenty-one audience members filled out response cards and twenty-five to thirty-five audience members stayed at the end of each performance to participate in the talkback sessions. The talkback sessions after each performance included the actors and playwright in addition to invited panel participants. These invited guests included two local history teachers, a Cree educator who was also on the provincial history curriculum revision committee, and an Anishinaabe artist-scholar.

Vignette 3: Reconciliation! (2018–19)

The third vignette focuses on the experiences of Jennifer, an elementary music teacher, as she worked with her students on exploring the educational

Calls to Action in the TRC through the creation of a school musical: *Reconciliation!* This vignette illustrates a school-community-university partnership. After attending an Image Theatre Professional Development Workshop at McGill University in the fall of 2018, Jennifer and I spoke about the possibility of bringing together community members, artists, and research assistants to co-create a production with her grade 5 and 6 students around the TRC's educational Calls to Action. This initial conversation led to collaboration among Lisa, Tom, Nina, Barbara, students, staff, administration, parents, research assistants, and members of the Lester B. Pearson School Board, who all worked together to support the creation and performance of *Reconciliation!* This effort did not go unnoticed, as CTV News coverage of the event further documented this endeavour and members of the school board paid for all of their grade 5 students to be bussed to the school where the performance took place.

About This Book

Table 1.1 and the brief introduction to each of the vignettes are intended to provide an overview of the key participants and activities that took place within each endeavour. Chapter 3 will return to these descriptions and provide additional details about each vignette and the methodological underpinnings of the research projects. The cross-cutting themes include appropriation, embodiment, and centring the self within communities of practice.

Prior to this, chapter 2 will focus on curriculum theorizing, teacher agency, and the creation of a character in drama education and theatre contexts, in which the actor is often directed to bracket the subjective self. The issue with bracketing the subjective self, when engaging with the TRC and conversations around reconciliation, will be explored in relation to concerns such as appropriation and the problem and potential for harm to marginalized peoples and communities when an actor uncritically "walks in someone else's shoes."

Chapter 4 connects the cross-cutting themes from the vignettes with this theoretical conversation and then discusses the emergent themes of risk, belonging, and counter-narratives. Reframing risk as a needed rupture (or crack) that will let the "light" in is theorized before discussing how belonging, being, and affect help one to consider subjectivity in a new way. The chapter concludes with counter-narratives as a starting point for informing unsettling pedagogies of hope and emergent acts of reconciliation.

Chapter 5 offers new directions for models for learning to engage with reconciliation praxis.

Image 1.4. Jennifer introducing *Reconciliation!* Photo taken by the author.

Chapter Two

Walk a Mile in Someone Else's Shoes: Situating Theories and Methods

Identity, Subjectivity, and Posthumanism

There is a liberal fantasy in which identities are merely chosen, so we are all free to be what we choose to be. But identities without demands would be useless to us. Identities work only because, once they get their grip on us, they command us, speaking to us as an inner voice; and because others, seeing who they think we are, call on us too.

Appiah, *The Lies That Bind* (2018, pp. 217–18)

There has been a sharp increase in interest related to studying and understanding the concept of identity dating back to the middle of the twentieth century in both sociology and psychology. In the domain of psychology, Erik Erikson published *Childhood and Society* in 1950, which was followed by *Identity and the Life Cycle* (1959), *Identity: Youth and Crisis* (1968), and *Dimensions of a New Identity* (1979). In his first book, he argued that identity had become a problem in America because of the super-identity the nation was trying to create as a reaction to immigration (Appiah, 2018). In 1957, Alvin Gouldner, a sociologist, wrote about what one's social identity meant in relation to participation within a group, and how this process often started with the question: Who is he? This question allowed others to categorize and pigeonhole an individual for the purposes of differing sets of expectations, rights, and obligations (as cited in Appiah, 2018). These early discussions on identity led to a plethora of domain-specific definitions and categorizations for identity, each based in specific cultural, social, historical, and political contexts. For example, a social identity places an individual within a certain social structure, where the influence of ideas such as a national identity implicate an individual's social role within a larger and interconnected reality.

Conversely, a personal identity can be viewed as multiple, evolving, and related to one's personal habits, experiences, and history. The complex interactions between identities (i.e., sexuality, gender, class, ability) led to the popularization of the term "intersectionality" by Kimberlé Crenshaw, a feminist legal theorist, in 1991. The implication that intersectionality has had on identity is to acknowledge that each person has multiple and overlapping identities. Arguably, this means that there can be no guarantee that any two people can ever have the same understandings based on an experience.

Appiah (2018) takes up the conversation on the construction of identity by proposing that there are three important discoveries that have emerged in relation to identity research. These are (1) habitus, the centrality of identity in relation to how we deploy our bodies; (2) essentialism, how we classify people into categories; and (3) clannishness, preferring our own kind, rather than belonging to humankind. Appiah goes onto discuss how these three concepts construct and affect personal identity in its connection to a complex and collective network of religious, national, racial, class-based, and cultural contexts. The metaphor of different identities being masks that one wears at different times reveals how identities become compartmentalized in response to context. Depending on the circumstance one is in, the same individual can be a kind, caring, and compassionate brother/father/teacher or a power-hungry boss/patriarch/partner. These identity-masks become a part of daily life as one moves between home, work, and social life, and they act as both barriers and passageways within various domains.

Subjectivity is also relevant to discussions on identity. Subjectivity means that, although a group of teachers may link a part of their identities to being teachers, each individual will have a different emotional and physical reaction to life experiences. Ellis and Flaherty (1992) suggest that subjectivities are "the human lived experience and the physical, political and historical context of that experience" (p. 75). This means that "thoughts, feelings, opinions and reactions are subjective [and] subjectivities can be regarded as the ways we perceive, feel and express ourselves" (Wales, 2009, as cited in Carter, 2014a, p. 2).

In *Beyond the Masks: Race, Gender and Subjectivity*, Amina Mama (1995) argues for the need to look at one's racialized and gendered identities to move towards a radically different notion of subjectivity. Subjectivity or "individuality and self-awareness – the condition of being a subject" (Henriques et al., 1984, p. 83 as cited in Mama, 1995) is favoured by Mama as a way of rejecting the psychological use of the term "identity" because of the way that "identity" creates internal (personal) and external (social) territories. Focusing on subjectivity over identity to understand one's experiences resonates with discussions around inter-subjectivity and agency in drama and theatre education (Wright, as cited in Schonmann, 2011). In drama and theatre, actors work on developing self-awareness physically and emotionally (Benedetti, 1976; Stanislavski, 1989) so that they can create a character and then work with fellow actors on a production (Weigler, 2001) before returning to the outside world (Courtney, 1986). Despite differences in terms, Appiah (2018) asserts:

> If you do not care for the shapes your identities have taken, you cannot simply refuse them; they are not yours alone. You have to work with others inside and outside the labeled group in order to reframe them so they fit you better; and you can do that collective work only if you recognize that the results must serve others as well. (p. 218)

This statement resonates with the intentions of the research presented in this book because it shows how care for one's identity and the implications of agency on oneself and others are essential. It also shows that collective work is relational and must take place in the service of a greater good. This means that rather than making a hard delineation to focus on subjectivity over identity or vice versa, it is important to be mindful of the context of ongoing development. This discussion on subjectivity and identity can be connected to conversations on "being," where being is understood as a verb that means we are always in a process of becoming, a process that requires belonging and being-in-relationship-with (Nancy, 2000). This phenomenon of being contends that there is no meaning if meaning is not shared, and not because there would be an ultimate or first signification that all beings have in common, but because meaning is itself the sharing of being (Nancy, 2000, p. 2). There is circulation in meaning, and we are all part of that circulation.

Furthermore, posthumanists contend that there is a need to "devise new social, ethical and discursive schemes of subject formation to match the profound transformations we are undergoing [because] the posthuman condition urges us to think critically and creatively about who and what we are actually in the process of becoming" (Braidotti, 2013, p. 12). This focus is informed by the ways that posthumanism interrogates the cybernetic triangle of human/animal/machine in the humanities and social sciences, and by "the emergence of an object-oriented ontology (OOO) that moves beyond the cybernetic triangle toward a flat ontology" (Snaza et al., 2014, p. 40). The Eurocentric paradigm that institutional and pedagogical practices are structured around – where subjectivity is related to consciousness, rationality, and with the human as the centre – is no longer the axis around which everything else pivots (Braidotti, 2013,

2017, 2019; Snaza et al., 2014). As new materialisms also argue, "there is no definitive break between sentient and nonsentient entities or between material and spiritual phenomena" (Coole & Frost, 2010, p. 10). This orientation "conceives of matter itself as lively or as exhibiting agency" (p. 9) and resists dualisms, binaries, and dialectical reconciliation by espousing a "monological account of emergent, generative material being" (p. 8).

Conceiving matter as possessing its own modes of self-transformation, self-organization, and directedness, and thus no longer as simply passive or inert, disturbs the conventional sense that agents are exclusively humans, who possess the cognitive abilities, intentionality, and freedom to make autonomous decisions. It also disrupts the corollary presumption that humans have the right or ability to master nature. Instead, the human species is being relocated within a natural environment whose material forces themselves manifest agentic capacities and in which the domain of unintended or unanticipated effects is considerably broadened (Coole & Frost, 2010, p. 10).

One of the central premises of posthumanism is that the subject is viewed as immanent and not transcendent. The subject is a being that can be-come through education and is not a being that "is." In part one of Rosi Braidotti's Tanner Lecture at Yale University (2017) entitled "Memoirs of a Post-Humanist," she presents her cartographic explanation for how the posthuman subject is a materially embedded, multilayered, inter-relational, temporal, nomadic entity. This subject, she argues, is one of immanence as considered by theorists such as Spinoza, Foucault, and Deleuze, rather that one of transcendence as in the works of Kant, Derrida, and Levinas. The post-feminist, critical, multilayered lens from which this understanding of the subject emerges means that we are always in the process of becoming(s) in a future-past time continuum. As we cease to be in the virtual and actual, we are simultaneously in a relational process of becoming in multidirectional ways in the posthuman present.

For Higgins and Madden (2019), the posthuman turn that decentres both the human and Western humanism problematizes where posthumanisms are situated because they "contend that this positioning risks subsuming or suturing over the ways in which Indigenous ways-of-knowing- in-being have been thinking and practicing co-constitutive relations to other-than- and more-than-human worlds since time immemorial, and thus differentially (re)producing (neo-) colonial relations" (see Bang & Marin, 2015; Todd, 2016; Watts, 2013, as cited in Higgins & Madden, 2019, p. 295). This critique is significant because it can also be tricky for settlers and newcomers to work from a decolonizing framework, prompting questions such as "Do I reject a settler future (Tuck & Yang, 2012) as a part of this undertaking?" Smith (1999) describes how "[t]he binary of colonizer/colonized does not take into account ... the development of different layering which have occurred within each group and across the two groups" (p. 27). This suggests that the imagined construction of whiteness that has been perpetuated through the process of colonization has homogenized a diverse group of white ethnic groups into a single entity for the purposes of domination (Leonardo, 2004). If the settler and the colonized are both constructions, can decolonizing methodologies that "evoke collective hope instead of individual blaming" (Diversi & Moreira, 2009, p. 207) be appropriately and respectfully used by settlers to work towards dismantling structures of colonization?

Barad's (2014) work on agential realism and intra-acting with diffraction offers an opportunity to not only reflect on something but also to continually turn it over again and again. Turning questions, positions, and views over and over again leads one to view a situation/question/story/problem as ongoing, evolving, and unique to the people, place(s), times, and conversations that are lived. It also means that there can be no single view of nationhood and national identity, which are also important constructs that have been a part of Canada's colonial agenda.

> Nation building has been the main theme of Canada's history curricula for a long time, and Aboriginal peoples, with a few notable exceptions, have been portrayed as bystanders, if not obstacles, to that enterprise ... Beginning in the 1980s, the history of Aboriginal people was sometimes cast in a more positive light, but the poverty and social dysfunction in Aboriginal communities were emphasized without any historical context to help students understand how or why these happened. This has left most Canadians with the view that Aboriginal people were and are to blame for the situations in which they find themselves, as though there were no external causes. Aboriginal peoples have therefore been characterized as a social and economic problem that must be solved. By the 1990s, textbooks emphasized the role of Aboriginal peoples as protestors, advocating for rights. Most Canadians failed to understand or appreciate the significance of these rights. (Madden, 2019, p. 287)

As Ahluwalia et al. (2012) and Regan (2010) contend, pedagogical and curricular work needs to take place in order to challenge nationalistic "truth-myths" (a term coined by Donald, 2012), or idealized versions of history. These are made simple and coherent in their reference to true experiences for dominant group members, and then they morph into hegemonic expressions of existing value structures and worldviews of the dominant groups. This needs to be done so that "welcoming the cultural other [no longer means perpetuating] the violence of Settler colonialism and the dominance of white Euro-descendant peoples in Settler society" (Kerr & Andreotti, 2017; see also Mackey, 2002; St. Denis,

2011). As Kerr (2019) proposes, it is the denial of relationality that needs to be a key target of settler re-education, and so moving towards a relational ontology is an important aspect of this unfolding research.

Currere *and Phenomenology*

Humanity does not gradually progress from combat to combat until it arrives at universal reciprocity, where the rule of law finally replaces warfare; humanity installs each of its violences in a system of rules and thus proceeds from domination to domination.

Michel Foucault, *Language, Counter-Memory, Practice* (1977, p. 151)

I have spent the last thirteen years teaching and researching the experiences of pre- and in-service teachers. A part of this work has been to explore how individuals arrive at choosing teaching as their profession. While answers to this query vary, each time I ask "Why did you want to become a teacher?" a significant number of people respond by describing teaching as their calling (Palmer, 2007), as something they always knew they wanted to do. Many of these people have integrity and are willing to sacrifice their own time and money for the good of their students as a contribution to society. They are courageous because they must continually overcome their own fears about administrative pressures, political evils, and how much they know about their subject matter (Palmer, 2007) in order to inspire, teach, encourage, and challenge the learners in their midst. This ethos of care is then met by low wages, little classroom support for differentiation, public criticism, and scapegoating (Carvel, 2000). As a result, the teaching profession has one of the worst retention rates of the professions and when students do not perform well on provincial tests, teachers and individual schools are held accountable. There is a clash between a teacher's personal identity and the identity that is held in society about the teaching profession.

Perhaps, as Madeleine Grumet argues in *Bitter Milk* (1988), this disproportionate level of public mistrust for teachers and the teaching profession stems from the process of distancing children from the care, love, and emotional support that they ideally begin their lives with through parental relationships. This happens as the needs of society to turn children into particular kinds of people who do particular kinds of work eclipse the innate dispositions of kindness, compassion, and empathy in order to create competitive, standardized, driven "people" who are more suited to taking orders and achieving economic benefits. This act of violence affects nearly everyone and everything our planet. As I argue in *Imagination: Hope for a Severed Curriculum* (Carter, 2014b), creative, emotionally engaged communities of people who care to counteract the trends of glo-balization, neo-liberalism, and capitalism are needed if change is to take place, despite the strength of the systems of oppression that have been embedded hegemonically in society. How does the farce of meritocracy (Sensoy & DiAngelo, 2011) still persist in North America? Is it even eth-ical to ask teachers to provoke their students to critically and creatively think about the world (Lecun & Hollister, 2017) when versions of success seem to continually come back to the importance of corporations' bottom lines (Isaksen & Akkermans, 2011) over communities (Greene, 1995)? We might agree that one important goal of education is to prepare students for the society within which they live, but what if society is wrong?

Yet, within this dangerous and debilitating climate some teachers are still trying to bring social justice content and conversations into their classrooms because they are committed to positive future change and the generations of children who will one day hold this world in their hands. They quietly go about their mandated tasks and act as champions for change by opening up spaces for topics, programs, and conversations that challenge the status quo. As a way of supporting new drama teachers navigating the demanding requirements of the profession, my disserta-tion work (Carter, 2014a) focused on the use of the method of *currere*.

William Pinar first introduced *currere*, or "the running of a course," in 1974, and then discussed it with Madeline Grumet as a method for systematic educational self-study in 1975. This method has four steps: regressive, progressive, analytical, and synthetical. The regressive step considers one's past lived experiences as data. This information is self-selected by the individual using free association to revisit a memory that they may later wish to reframe. I have often suggested in my teaching that students use a difficult educational moment as a starting place for this regressive stage and that they recall this moment in as much detail as possible. In the progressive step one then looks at what does not yet exist and imagines possible futures. This hopeful space allows the in-dividual to consider what could happen differently in a similar future situation. In the analytical stage, one examines the past and the future si-multaneously to create a subjective space of freedom in the present. The synthetical moment is an opportunity to ask: What is the meaning of the present? Engaging in the process of *currere* is meant to help an individual address a significant and personal educational moment by dynamically and psychoanalytically looking at it in order to understand the roots of the issue. By following this method, one can deepen agency "because au-tobiography is concerned with reconstructing self and cultivating singu-larity, which is politically progressive and psychologically self-affirmative" (Pinar, 1975 as cited in Kumar, 2013 p. 10).

For many years, I used the four-step *currere* process with drama education students, including those who participated in the research described
in Vignette 1 (see chapter 1). As a part of this work, students were asked
to think of an educational moment from their own teaching experiences
to revisit, reframe, and reimagine using the monologue[1] as the format
for the process. When the problematic moment was shared with the audience, a post-performance conversation about emerging insights from the
synthetical stage took place. Using the *currere* process and its theoretical
underpinnings to understand and frame students' experiences as they created and performed monologues worked well until the students wanted
to create characters based on someone else's experiences. The reason that
this caused tension (in Vignette 1) is that classroom conversations were
focused on taking on roles of people who did not have the same lived/
embodied experiences. One student named this process "appropriation."
This led to a debate about Appiah's (2018) contention that "if you do not
care for the shapes your identities have taken, you cannot simply refuse
them; they are not yours alone" and the idea of drama education as a
curricular space for exploring "walking in someone else's shoes." The tensions that arose from these conversations are discussed further in the next
chapter as a part of the theme "appropriation and embodiment."

Pragmatically, these concerns led to a phenomenological framing
of the devised theatre processes in *Sing the Brave Song: This Isn't Over!*
and in *Reconciliation!* (Carter & Mreiwed, 2017). Phenomenology was
a pragmatic decision because it considers how consciousness relates to
first-person subjectivities and why/how one perceives things to understand them (Cerbone, 2006; Heidegger, 1962; Husserl, 1965; Kant, 1965;
Merleau-Ponty, 1964; Moustakas, 1994; Sartre, 1992; Van Manen, 1990,
2014). Bracketing the subjective self as a part of the phenomenological
reduction provides a viable way to account for the creation of a character (see Image 2.1) because when an actor creates a character, they are
"bracketing" their own thoughts, experiences, likes, dislikes, ideals and
embodied experiences to become the scripted character that they are to
portray on stage or screen.

In Vignettes 2 and 3, the participants followed the three steps of the
phenomenological reduction when creating their characters. These
three steps, in relation to the work described in the vignettes, and how

---

1 A monologue is a dramatic convention in which one performer speaks directly to the
   audience about their inner thoughts on a specific issue or topic. The use of the monologues with pre-service teachers is a convention used in *The Teacher Monologues: Exploring the Identities and Experiences of Artist-Teachers* (Carter, 2014a) that offers the potential
   for both transformation and illumination of an education moment.

Image 2.1. Phenomenological reduction (used as a theoretical guide for understanding the process of subjective bracketing during the creation of a character, and the impact of this process on identity, but not as a systematic method for analysis).

this work may be taken up with pre-and in-service teachers interested in using the arts to explore the TRC, are as follows:

Step 1: Learn about the educational Calls to Action in the TRC and connect this information to one's own intellectual and experiential positions. This process took place as an exercise in learning together, where students engaged with a variety of texts, including survivor testimonies. This work was facilitated by Alayna in Vignette 2 and Jennifer in Vignette 3. Participants' direct perceptions and personal engagements with the information that they learned about in this step arguably affected their consciousnesses, as indicated by Jesse:

> I thought I knew a lot. I took a Canadian history class in university and learned a bit in high school. Then, coming into the rehearsal process and seeing the script and interacting with the script, I'm learning more and more every day. It's making me more cognisant of everything that's going on, as well. Like, someone made a comment about some Indigenous people at the Atwater metro station and how they were a disturbance for them. I was like, "Wait, what?" and instead of brushing this off I engaged in this conversation and challenged this comment, so it's changing things for me, and not just in the rehearsal room.

Step 2: In this step of the phenomenological reduction, one brackets the subjective self in order to return to and focus on one's experience with a thing/event/topic. In this context, the actor brackets their subjectivity in order to create a character with a different lived experience. Because of the devised natures of *Sing the Brave Song: This Isn't Over!* and *Reconciliation!* this step also became a collaborative and dialogic engagement.

Step 3: In phenomenology, this step is meant to capture the new understanding of the topic/issue explored in Step 1, as a result of the subjective bracketing process in Step 2.

  These three steps build on the premise that one should bracket the subjective self (i.e., walk in someone else's shoes) as a part of the character creation process. This phenomenological approach resonates with a relational and postmodern view of identity because phenomenologists consider consciousness to be relational. Edmund Husserl (1859–1938) was the principal founder of phenomenology. His idea of consciousness, in relation to the philosophy of phenomenology and its historical importance for our discussions on identity, highlights how at the heart of phenomenology is first of all a rejection of metaphysics and academic philosophy. This is the meaning of his famous slogan "Back to the things themselves." It is not just a method of doing philosophy but also an attitude of mind. When Husserl told his students they should get back to the things themselves, what he meant was that he was not interested in what they knew about philosophy, what they had learned at school or university, but whether they could talk philosophically about what they saw in front of them – a table, for example (Large, 2008, p. 4).

  Husserl and the history of phenomenology is relevant to this book because "getting back to the things themselves" reminds us that there is no amount of studying or knowledge that we can acquire about something that can make up for personal experience, despite the difficulty of observing what is closest to us precisely. What follows is not to ask "Where does a word come from?" as though this was doing philosophy, but "Does this word help me understand what I am seeing?" For example, when looking at a tree, I do not just see something, I see something as something (i.e., never the tree, but always the tree *as* a tree). Contained in this "as" is the meaning of Husserl's intentionality, which requires us to stop thinking of consciousness as an empty sack that one takes out into the world and fills with experience. Husserl tells us that consciousness is already outside of itself, already related to things in the world. The world is not something out there; rather, we are our world. This means that one cannot understand consciousness if one refers to some kind of mysterious thing like the "I" or the "self." Consciousness is only a relation. Consciousness is always consciousness of something, never just consciousness.

  There are two things in this discussion that bear significance on the conversations in this book. First, thinking of consciousness as a relation and not a part of the "I" is important when considering Appiah's (2018) descriptions of identity. Second, intentionality imbedded within the use of "as" is important in helping to frame understandings of truth and reconciliation projects because if one's intention in engaging with reconciliation is always bound together with seeing "a tree as a tree" there can be no recognition of the multiple "truths" that need to coexist within relations of understandings. What is important are not claims about reality, but how consciousness experiences the world. "There is not a subject and object separate from one another, which then, through some kind of unexplainable and unknowable process, have to become linked or attached. Rather, they are already intertwined in our direct experience in the world. This is what is meant by 'consciousness'" (Large, 2008, p. 5). Moving from Husserl's view of consciousness requires the inclusion of a description of Being.[2] For Martin Heidegger (1889–1976), Being is presupposed in phenomenology. To get at the meaning of Being, we need to philosophically consider it through phenomenology by approaching this concern with a new question: What is the meaning of Being itself? The challenge with approaching such a problem philosophically is knowing how to ask the question. This harkens back to the key notions of intentionality and the kind of consciousness it presupposes:

> But why should we, first of all, be thought of in terms of consciousness? Does this way of relating to the world sum up who or what we are, and is it the only way in which we relate to the world? It is not only that traditional phenomenology does not have answers to these questions, but it does not even ask them. It takes for granted that we are nothing but "consciousness," and being conscious is directly understood through intentionality as objectivity. (Large, 2008, p. 9)

Even though Husserl, like Descartes and Kant, understands the Being of the object through the subject, its Being is in fact only interpreted through this relation. The subject vanishes in the very objectivity of knowledge. Heidegger goes onto say that throughout phenomenology

---

2 The distinction between "being" and "Being" in German is easy because they have a grammatical difference. "Being," *Sein*, means existence, and "being" is *Seiende*, which means "a being." In English, being is understood as something which exists; while Being denotes existence. The problem with Being relates to its definition alongside Heidegger's *Dasein* (i.e., there is only one being that is important to our consideration of Being, and that is ourselves), which contends that humans are more significant than other beings because we are the only beings for whom the question of Being can be a question (i.e., humans seek an answer to questions about their existence – Who am I? What I am doing?). Heidegger calls this a fundamental ontology, and he suggests that we exist because we have an understanding of our Being as the very basis of our Being (Large, 2008).

one must have the courage to accept what is really seen in the phenomenon precisely as it presents itself, rather than interpreting it away, and
honestly describe it. Having *the courage to accept what is really seen* is an
important ethical guideline when considering how to narratively consider the data within each of the vignettes, because one must understand
how the relational consciousness of the participants working together
affected the intentionality of the work being done. And so a component
of this research began with a focus on testing the bracketing of the subject self-process to determine not only if a participant could "see something as if for the first time" through the creation of a character, but if
they should. Further to this point are the foundational assumptions that
support this thesis, that humans can be defined by their minds, and that
the fundamental ontology of phenomenology is predicated on separating humans from non-humans. The first concern was complicated by
emphasizing the embodied nature of existence when Husserl revealed
the importance of the lifeworld, Heidegger added equipment, Levinas
added the other, de Beauvoir added gender, and Merleau-Ponty added
the body (Lewis & Owen, 2020).

However there is a tendency in phenomenology to stay within the
human-centric research paradigm. In "Posthuman Phenomenologies:
Performance Philosophy, Non-Human Animals, and the Landscape"
Lewis and Owen (2020) contend that in order explore the possibilities
of the posthuman in phenomenology for unsettling human centredness,
forms of performance philosophy are needed to allow for the exploration of new and needed terrain that disrupts the intellectualism that
haunts Western philosophy. They describe how imaginative speculation
can lead to embodied aesthetic entanglements that allow for productive change that challenges the boundaries of space and communication
between the human and non-human. Rather than imagining what the
other feels, they seek to feel what the other feels, as a way of performing
the posthuman.

For Clement (2017), post-humanist phenomenology (Escobar, 2007;
Lyotard, 1991; Sundberg, 2013) offers a way to destabilize colonial ways
of thinking. Clement describes how the Maori *haka* is a holistic discourse
that demonstrates an embodiment of the principle of equality, and of
reciprocity between Maori and their environment. The *haka* exemplifies
the obligations of respect, guardianship, and enhancement humans owe
to the natural world (Henry & Pene, 2001, 236; Mika, 2015, 63; Patterson, 1994, 399–400, 404; Roberts et al., 2004). For both Clément (2016)
and Lewis and Owen (2020), a common characteristic of posthuman
phenomenology is the significance of an in-between space of emergence
or becoming. This liminal space is needed to allow one to explore, try

out, practise, and express connection. Such spaces are prerequisites for teacher education programs working towards reconciliation praxis and pedagogy (Hare, 2020 & Brant-Birioukov et al., 2020, as cited in Phelan et al., 2020).

Contexts

Section 8.1 of the Quebec drama education curriculum describes how students are required to create characters as a way of representing their inner images in different ways and in various contexts as an expression of a sociocultural reality. There are numerous ways that actors create characters. Some begin with asking themselves questions: Who am I? Where am I? Where am I going? Other acting methods focus on the use of objectives, stakes, and obstacles for character development (Benedetti, 2008). The body and voice are yet one more starting point (i.e., physical acting approaches) to begin this process (Droznin, 2016). Regardless of the exact approach or combination of approaches that one uses during character development, the admonition, *walk a mile in someone else's shoes*, is consistently referred to. This phrase means that before judging someone else (or in this case becoming someone else vis-à-vis a character), you must understand their experiences, challenges, and thought processes as fully as possible.

In each of the vignettes, participants developed characters and/or built their plays around their inquiries about the TRC's educational Calls to Action. These personal engagements demanded physical, intellectual, emotional, and sometimes metaphysical work.

New ideas, questions, and perspectives became relevant because the experiences of others became a part of their own narratives as they actively worked to address and explore together. This illustrates how drama and theatre-creation processes are steps that can lead to an understanding of how to shift an individual's perceptions, emotions, or creative engagements in thoughtful and proactive ways, often by developing a character or portraying one. Through this connection with the other – with the world – both in mind and body, one is able to feel a situation through a bodily affect before being deliberately rational about it. The arts consider the following as essential to learning: (1) the environment in which learning takes place; (2) materials and curriculum that help learners to notice the world; (3) teacher scaffolding to promote learning that leads to independence; and (4) assessments that can be examined in social and not individual terms. Arts-based educational research (ABER) is used to underpin this research methodologically.

Arts-Based Educational Research (ABER)

Although ABER has been extensively theorized, used, and written about, definitive guideposts for prescriptive approaches to "doing" ABER are often counter to this methodology making it difficult to systematically analyse and conceptually consider arts-based data beyond mere description. In the interest of delving more deeply into a conceptual analysis of the data from the research projects presented in this book, the larger umbrella of qualitative research is referred to in order to situate ABER, narrative inquiry, and the subsequent analysis of data. Qualitative methods rely on "text and image data, have unique steps in data analysis, and draw on diverse designs" (Creswell, 2014, p. 183). In qualitative research, the intent of the research is important, as is the role of the researcher. Depending on the methods selected, there are a variety of steps for analysing, ensuring validity, and documenting accuracy (Creswell, 2014). Some of the basic characteristics of a qualitative study include the following: the data being collected takes place in a natural setting; the researcher is a key instrument in collecting data through interviews, observation, so on, and in analysing it; multiple sources of data are used to gather information; the data analysis process is inductive to begin with; the research design is often emergent; researcher reflexivity may affect the direction of the study; and research is often holistic. Since these key characteristics are all aspects of the research described in this book, the overarching methodology of the research projects can be described as qualitative. However, in order to allow for a more fluid relationship with the data, its representation, and its analysis, ABER is a complement to this overarching design. That said, there are also concerns to be aware of. Lynn Butler-Kisber (2010, pp. 12–21) defines the main considerations for engaging in qualitative research as trustworthiness, particularizability, access and consent, reflexivity, voice, and transparency. After her definitions, I lay out my response to these considerations, below:

• *Trustworthiness* – Trustworthiness is the confidence a reader can place in the productive truths contained in this research and how this can be derived from a number of factors. First, with over twenty years of experience teaching drama and theatre in three countries at the K–University levels, I have a clear understanding of the implications of using the arts to provoke dialogical conversations on critical societal issues from political, professional, and personal levels. Second, by providing my own story in the research and with participants, I reflexively situate interactions and clarify both how and why I came to my interpretations of the data. Finally, trustworthiness came through a triangulation of methods through multiple forms of data collection with participants, by regularly engaging in participant verification, and by analysing, coding, and interpreting data with a team of RAs.

- *Particularizability* – The results presented are particularizable to the context of this research because they resonate with the participants in addition to confirming and producing new understandings of their experiences.
- *Access and consent* – Inquiry must be done with a keen sensitivity to the participants' and the research sites' needs, as well as an ongoing dialogue on consent. Prior to engaging in research, I obtained ethical approval from the McGill Research Ethics Board Office and the additional sites where the research was conducted. This process included the option of using a pseudonym and later gave participants the opportunity to verify research texts before dissemination to ensure accuracy when possible.
- *Reflexivity* – To account for my identity, assumptions and biases, I verbally situate myself throughout the research creation processes with participants prior to working with them. I also share my own positionality at the start of this book, in addition to the ongoing reflexive relationship I have with my emergent understandings over time.
- *Voice* – Rather than seeking to objectively portray participants' experiences, I opt to deliberately include, as often as possible, the particularities of individual experience by using participants' own words. Though ultimately I am the curator of the stories in this book, I have sought to include a significant quantity of quotes from the participants to allow greater voice, and recognition of the ways that the understandings in this book are a result of participants' words, ideas, and understandings I also consciously attempt to resist using overly academic jargon throughout this book because I believe that knowledge and information should not be a privilege for only highly educated people to engage in.
- *Transparency* – Finally, this work seeks transparency by situating ethical and relational dimensions of the work first. As previously discussed, I begin by situating myself as a member of McGill University, who grew up primarily in northwestern Ontario with various experiences as a child and youth that have affected my views of myself and the world.

As Butler-Kisber (2010) argues, there is no "recipe" for qualitative research, but the issues presented above are "integral to the work and require attention throughout any inquiry process" (p. 22). This means that ongoing attention to them is an important aspect of this research framework and a consideration of the process of fostering social justice through creative teacher agency. Data analysis has also been undertaken by both myself and the research assistants using traditionally qualitative ways of conceptualizing approaches to analysis and interpretation. NVivo software was used for some parts of the project as a tool for managing and manipulating the material when larger data sets were being reviewed. However, NVivo had limitations for the conceptual analysis work, signalling a need to consider arts-based approaches as a way of honouring some of the creative data sets in this research.

Further to the classification of this research as qualitative, it could fit within a critical, constructivist, or even pragmatic philosophical paradigm. However, I have chosen to highlight the arts-based or aesthetic intersubjective stance attributed to ABER because it encompasses the belief system that intersects most closely with my own ontology. This means that "the arts are able to access that which is otherwise out of reach [and] value preverbal ways of knowing, including sensory, emotional, perceptual, kinesthetic, and imaginal knowledge" (Leavy, 2017, p. 14). In arts-based educational research, research is a relational, meaning-making activity that can still draw upon theories of embodiment, phenomenology, and additional perspectives.

Because drama and theatre are the primary focus for opening up curricular spaces to evoke new understandings, connections, and conversations within an educational context, ABER most closely aligns with the art and drama education curricular project that this research explores. Creating art provides an opportunity for communication and representation that can be unique because the arts allow for socio-emotional and embodied synthesis. Butler-Kisber (2010) suggests that qualitative inquiry can be subdivided into thematic, narrative, and arts-informed categories:

1 Thematic inquiry uses categorization as an approach (Maxwell & Miller, 2008) for interpretation that produces a series of themes that emerge in the process of the research that account for experiences across groups or situations;

2 Narrative inquiry uses a number of connecting approaches to produce a contextualized and contiguous interpretation and storied account(s) of the particular situation(s);

3 Arts-informed inquiry uses various forms of art to interpret and portray the focus of the particular study ... and can be carried out with participants in more or less participatory ways or can have a more inward and autobiographical [approach]. (p. 8)

These three categories (i.e., thematic inquiry, narrative inquiry, and arts-informed inquiry) can be separate categories or they can exist simultaneously. For example, a song could be an arts-based sample that tells a narrative on a theme. Although I would argue that it is a stretch to consider this an example of triangulation, it behoves researchers using ABER to create separations between categories of analysis simply to avoid the messiness that this kind of work elicits and necessitates. For this reason, thematic inquiry and narrative inquiry are the categorizations used to create themes as a part of the ongoing data analysis of the various texts used in this book.

A final note about the positioning of this research is in relation to the performative inquiry (PI) category (Fels, 1999) within ABER. PI, or the exploration of a topic through performance, is an additional ABER tradition within which there are multiple categorizations. These include approaches such as performative ethnography (Mienczakowski, 1995); ethnodrama (Saldana, 2008; Reader's Theatre (Donmoyer & Yennie-Donmoyer, 2008); Theatre of the Oppressed (Boal, 1979); research-based theatre (Belliveau, 2015); and play-building (Norris, 2000). Given the collective, emergent, and interconnected nature of this research, the larger category of ABER, and the specific narrative inquiry and narrative analysis areas nested within qualitative domains, best honour and represent the journey of the participants in this research.

Narrative Inquiry

Polkinghorne (1995) "distinguishes between qualitative studies that employ narrative analysis [as] studies whose data consist of actions, events, and happenings, but whose analysis produces stories (e.g., biographies, histories, case studies)" and studies that analyse narratives, "studies whose data consist of narratives or stories, but whose analysis produces paradigmatic typologies or categories [e.g., thematic]" (as cited in Fischer, 2019, p. 23). This means that both narrative analysis and the analysis of narrative have an equal potential to generate the meta-narratives through arts-based exemplars (i.e., monologues, dramatic dialogues, audience talkback conversations, reflections during the creative process) that illustrate how drama education and theatre might be used to explore social justice topics and foster agency. Narrative analysis presents the research story in "a plot that ties together what happens and invites readers or listeners to evaluate the meanings of the actors' actions and decisions" (Bochner & Riggs, 2014, p. 205). This is a highly contextualized form of inquiry that relies on the power of story to build empathy, to examine individual perceptions of cause and effect, to connect with memory, to generate contextualized learning, and to create a space that allows the storyteller and audience to co-engage in the interpretation process and to construct new meanings from the text. Narrative analysis, or presenting research as a story, allows for the nuance between reading about how to drive standard and actually developing the muscle memory for finding the "sweet spot" of a clutch (Fischer, 2019). O'Connor, Fitzgerald, and Fitzgerald (1969) describe the difference as follows:

> When you can state the theme of a story, when you can separate it from the story itself, then you can be sure the story is not a very good one. The meaning of a story has to be embodied in it, has to be made concrete in it. A story is a way to say something that can't be said any other way, and it takes every word in the story to say what the meaning is. You tell a story because a statement would be inadequate. When anybody asks what a story is about, the only proper thing is to tell him is to read the story. The meaning of fiction is not abstract meaning but experienced meaning, and the purpose of making statements about the meaning of a story is only to help you to experience that meaning more fully. (p. 96)

As such, stories have the ability to generate empathy and to enable people to make both micro- and macro-level connections to the topics being explored (Fischer, 2019). Such narratives "bestow meaning as much as (they) recognize some of the possibilities of meaning that lie always in the seemingly tangled messiness of lived experience" (Leggo, 2008, p. 5). This suggestion creates a contradiction between the implication that stories are subjective and can always be told in another way and concerns around the retelling of particular stories, such as teachings by Elders, which should not be retold in part, because certain stories have an agency of their own (Rajan Datta, personal communication, 9 October 2019). Regardless of which view(s) one holds about the agency of individual stories and which ones should be told and retold (and by whom and to whom), there is neuroscientific evidence (Dubuc, 2002; Mastin, 2010) that supports the Ancient Greek technique known as *elaborative coding* for how the human mind is hardwired to remember stories differently than facts, numbers, names, and other abstract concepts. Fischer (2019) describes how this process works:

> Declarative memory, the network in the brain responsible for conscious memories, can be divided into two parts: episodic memory for events and stories, and semantic memory for knowledge (e.g., the capitals of countries, phone numbers, names, etc.). Episodic "story" memory, in which "you see yourself as an actor in the events you remember" (Dubuc, 2002, Episodic

memory, para. 2), underpins semantic memory. Only through associations with episodic memory can generalizations be made into semantic memory (Mastin, 2010, Episodic & Semantic Memory, para. 3). For this reason, people from Ancient Greece through to modern memory champions have all relied on story as a mnemonic; we are biologically hardwired to experience first and then to make abstractions after. (p. 25)

Having chosen an art-based method to foster an environment for participants to learn from, engage with, create community though, and elicit responses from the audience, I opted for a narrative analysis that pays attention to literary and artistic elements such as point of view, character, tensions, and theme. For these reasons, qualitative and arts-based narrative analysis form the basis of this research.

Vignettes and Constant Comparison for Data Analysis

Further to the classification of this research as arts-based educational qualitative research that uses narrative inquiry and analysis, the narrative vignettes are classified as case studies. Although there are both prevalence and uncertainty about its nature and proper usage (Merriam, 1998), "case study," according to Yin (1994), "investigates a contemporary phenomenon within its real-world context" (p. 13) and is "an intensive, holistic description and analysis of a single instance, phenomenon or social unit" (Merriam, 1988, p. 21) that has boundaries. The purpose for naming the vignettes as case studies is that the data collected (interviews, photos, video recordings, and journal reflections) is bounded within the case study parameters: individual research questions, time-frames, main participants, and specific theatre-creation processes that took place within individual sites. The "particularistic and bounded" nature of the phases of the projects allowed for a focus on these specifications so that the findings from each case study could be used for future analysis across the vignettes using constant comparison (Maykut & Morehouse, 1994) and could inform further understandings. Because ABER allows for a lot of flexibility as a methodological approach, the specifications of the case study and its bounded nature allowed for the creation of enabling constraints (Sumara & Davis, 2006) for analysis.

Constant comparison is an approach to research that allows for early assigning of descriptive labels and codes. Once these often thematic codes are assigned, they can be defined, categorized, and collapsed to move data into more conceptual domains with common elements in order to reveal deeper connections (Strauss & Corbin, 1990). The constant comparison of data across the vignettes took place both in recognition of my own recursive researcher stance as a complement to the multiple research assistants who took part in the collection of data in the field and the conversations that we had when thinking about the data in specific cases.

The initial analysis of the data generated was in response to the research questions. After the completion of each of the projects, the relevant data (i.e., interviews, focus groups) was transcribed and then categorized into a shared Google Docs folder in my research lab. Data was also put into NVivo and initial themes were considered. Since each phase of each project was informed and connected to the others, ongoing analyses and constant comparison across case studies naturally took place. After detailed descriptions of each case study were written, a conceptual analysis of the data took place, followed by concept mapping of the cross-vignette themes, as a way of zooming out (Bochner & Riggs, 2014) from the individual stories in order to consider larger implications of the research. The value of this methodological approach to the reader lies in the practical drama and theatre examples that the pre- and in-service teachers and participants used to explore the TRC, and in the ways that this approach allowed for participant meaning-making to be represented.

Making Sense of the Data, Saturation, and Validity

Given the large data set (in relation to a singular qualitative case study), cross-study colour coded themes of individual vignettes were created so that the frequency of the themes in relation to key words could be visualized. After this initial process, the vignettes were rewritten with the intention of telling a larger story related to how creative teacher agency might foster social and pedagogical justice. These narratives were shared with the participants for feedback to ensure that they agreed with the interpretations.

Chapter Three

We Start Here: Narratives, Vignettes, and Analysis

Narratives

Stories can be bad, bitter medicine and inspire people to bad actions; they can be used to separate us, fragment us into pieces, leave us bleeding and alone. Disconnection is cause and consequence of much of this world's suffering. We are disconnected from one another, from the plants and animals and elements upon which our survival depends, from ourselves and our histories and our legacies. When we don't recognize or respect our interdependencies, we don't have the full context that's necessary for healthy or effective action. Yet stories can be good medicine too. They can drive out the poison, heal the spirit as well as the body, remind us of the greatness of where we came from as well as the greatness of who we're meant to be, so that we're not determined by the colonial narrative of deficiency.

D.H. Justice, Why Indigenous Literatures Matter (2018, p. 4)

We are awash in stories. We are epistemologically and ontologically engaged in using stories as an integral way to sort out who we are as people in relation to other people. We are all creatively engaged in processes of identity formation and transformation by attending to stories. Everybody lives stories, all the time, and everybody attends to the stories of others.

C. Leggo, "Narrative Inquiry" (2008, p. 3)

My story. Your story. Our stories. Positioning this research as something that is trying to prove a research question so that results can be quantified, reproduced, and standardized would restrict the possibility of storying my story, your story, and our collective future stories. Created and shared meta-narratives are, as McNay (2009) points out, "not always readily acquired; important and relevant stories may never have been told, or told incompletely" (p. 2), and this is a risk inherent in storying our research and lives. But, as Fenske (2004) argues, aesthetic- or arts-based educational research is about constructing an invitation that does not predetermine appropriate interpretation but opens up a dialogic space of engagement (p.15). This invitation must be, and desire to be, unfinished. The reason for leaning into the idea of an unfinished story is that we can only understand and represent what we know at a particular time, and this changes. My story, your story, and our stories should be partial and they should change. They can be told and retold, formed and reformed. It is through the act of storying that we can create new stories that reshape who we are, who we want to be, and what we can collectively achieve.

After endless hours of writing and rewriting the vignettes, I still found it challenging to decide whose perspective to tell the stories from or how to restory the stories. Carl Leggo's article "Narrative Inquiry: Attending to the Art of Discourse" (2008) explains the three principle dynamics involved in narrative inquiry. These principles are story, interpretation, and discourse. Leggo argues that each of these principles is less about learning the correct recipe for telling a story and more about shaping and constructing a story for others. Instead of feeling overwhelmed by my mountain of data and "complain[ing] that there is something ridiculous about all the stars in the night sky, or all the species of plants, animals, fish, and insects in the earth" (p. 5), I began to see that restorying the narrative vignettes was an opportunity to delight in the beauty, abundance, and ways meaning-making can take place, leading to a semi-structured approach for starting the coarse ground analysis of the research data. This process is in line with Leggo's five step structure of reading the story, interrogating it, thematizing it, expanding it to look for possible meanings, and then summarizing the narrative for what has been learned. Although he uses this structure when introducing an approach to narrative analysis and interpretation, he also cautions the reader that by reducing analysis and interpretation to a paint-by-numbers type approach, we run the risk of reducing the complexities and ethical engagements embedded within stories. As a result, interpretation needs to be entered into with care, openness, and critique because as Clandinin and Connelly (2000) assert, narrative is both a phenomenon and method. As Justice (2018) discusses in *Why Indigenous Literatures Matter*, stories can also remind us "about who we are and where we're going, on our own and in relation to those with whom we share this world. They remind us about the relationships that make a good life possible" (p. 6). If, as Leroy Little Bear describes, Canada is a pretend nation that puts on costumes to take on new identities depending on context, we need to learn to listen to counter-stories that have been forgotten or suppressed because "teaching ... has to deal not so much with lack of knowledge as with resistances to knowledge" (Felman, 1982, p. 30).

In this chapter, discussions with and between participants from each of the vignettes, as well as excerpts from the scripts of *Sing the Brave Song: This Isn't Over!* and *Reconciliation!* are included. Some of the dialogues are verbatim, while others, such as the monologue below, use a compilation character to illustrate reoccurring themes within the vignettes. In this way, the monologue *I'm Still Canadian, Dad!* illustrates how arts-based educational research can be used to represent research findings through an artistic and storied form. The compilation character convention was used as a way for me to re-story and engage artistically with participant research data from *Sing the Brave Song: This Isn't Over!* using ABER methods. I performed this shortened version of *I'm Still Canadian, Dad!* at the McGill Artful Inquiry Research Group's 3rd Bi-Annual Symposium (Virtual) in October 2020. The reason for writing, rehearsing, and performing the research data in the form of this monologue is so that I as an artist-researcher can continue to engage artfully in the data collection, analysis, and dissemination phases.

Monologue: *I'm Still Canadian, Dad!*

My dad is so Canadian. So, you know, lovely.

He has always been kind and gentle and sees the world in this "do unto your neighbour as you would have them do unto you" kind of attitude. I mean, he opens doors for women and makes me walk on the inside of the pavement, so I won't get splashed by a car driving by if there are puddles. For him being Canadian means working hard, spending time with your family, and enjoying the simple things in life, like fishing in the summer and telling stories at a bonfire by the lake. Him and my mom have been married 40 years this fall, and they met in high school in the same small town that my great-grandparents came to as immigrants over 100 years ago. His father was in the Second World War and so my dad has always respected the whole legacy of what that means to this country. How his father fought for freedom and we need to keep our appreciation for the sacrifice of others alive in our collective consciousness. He cares. He really does.

[*CHUCKLES.*]

Do you remember those "I am Canadian" commercials in
the '90s? So, my brother, mom, and I happened to be
watching one of them at the same time when they first
came out and then just as the rant "aboot" Canadians being peacekeepers and not Americans "policing" the world
began, my dad walked in holding a Molson beer and wearing a plaid flannel shirt. Seriously!

We couldn't stop laughing! When my dad asked "what" we
were sent off into hysterics again. It was too perfect – and I
guess that's why I think of my dad as "so Canadian."

So honestly, I grew up in this great environment and
family that has always just felt like the typical Canadian
experience.

But then I moved away to go to school, and I was just, you
know, exposed to different ideas and peoples and perspectives. I don't know when it happened exactly, but I
was really interested in social justice issues and starting to
get involved in student government to try and improve
things. I became just more hyper aware about so many
things, but especially about what narratives were missing
in the collective Canadian conversation. I remember Kim
Campbell was asked, like to explain Canada's history to
the rest of the world in a "Being Canadian" show, and she
just said "Unknown." I even remember reading a book
called *The Brief History of Canada* and in the introduction
the first question asked was: What is Canada? What is a
Canadian?

Here I was thinking: You want to know what a Canadian is,
well, meet my dad! My dad is SO Canadian, end of story.
But then the book talked about this ongoing debate about
how trying to answer these questions has led to political,
intellectual, religious, and media-related debates. Some
nationalists suggested that we were a satellite of the US,
while others argued for a break from the French and English colonial legacies. Around the same time, I remember
reading a completely different take on the whole conversation by Leroy Little Bear. Bear called Canada a "Pretend
Nation" that has a costume trunk beside it because it so
quickly puts on the appropriate costume needed at a

particular time in history to appear in a certain way to others. This is contrasted to the Native way of thinking that he describes as a "symbiosis that developed between the land, the environment, and ecological aspects." It was about that relationship that affects knowledge and the embodied identities of people through stories, beliefs, and metaphysics.

Bear concludes:

So, if we look at Canada, it is not much different than a multi-billionaire whose wealth is strictly on paper. It is not connected to the land. It's like the person originally from San Francisco or Seattle, who then lived in Calgary for fifty or sixty years, and somebody asks, "Where are you from?" After fifty or sixty years of living in Calgary, the person answers, "I'm from San Francisco." Identity is being drawn elsewhere. So, it seems to me that if Canada were to be a true nation, it's going to have to embody the knowledge that has always been here. It's going to have to acknowledge its Aboriginal roots. Canada may have a constitution. Canada may have a government. Canada may have a legal system. But, just like that multibillionaire whose wealth exists entirely on paper, all of the above are simply a paper existence – not substantive in any sense. It doesn't arise from a mutual relationship with the totality of the ecology of territory.

[Pause.]

I know.

It kind of changes everything, right?

How would you explain that idea of "being Canadian" to my dad?

Fast-forward to being involved in this play – *Sing the Brave Song: This Isn't Over!* – and here I am looking at Indigenous issues framed through the lens of reconciliation – another, arguably, nationalistic construct. A lot of people have a lot of problems with this whole idea of "reconciliation."

Hey, no … don't get me wrong, I don't want to diminish the fact that in the production there are a lot of tough things that are explored and presented. One that comes to mind for me is the relationship between the police and Indigenous people – especially the lack of involvement by the police in relation to the missing and murdered Indigenous women and girls. But, I have police

in my family and my parents are coming to see the show
and so I am wondering if I should warn them about
some things or something. There are just all these tensions in moving between these evolving world views.
But at least we're trying to understand some of these
things ...

But, well, so I start to doubt myself and question, well,
EVERYTHING. And I ask myself, OK, so what would
I warn them about? What exactly? Wouldn't that just
be another way of playing into these ideas of white
fragility, where we don't want to hurt white people's
feelings? I know some of my aunts and uncles are always saying: "They just need to get over the past and
move on."

[*LOOKING AT THE AUDIENCE.*]

I know, you're thinking who says that? But it's true.

We think there are some random faceless people out there
who speak this way, but they aren't nameless or faceless. I
hear these conversations at the dinner table passed off as
jokes.

Maybe I have to warn everyone else about my family.

I wrote this monologue after using Leggo's five step structure to analyse the transcribed data from the second vignette. Once the data was analysed, the monologue form was used to explore the theme of "racism"
and how it plays out in different ways through Canadian settler views of
national identity. The monologue allowed for a turning over of the conversations between all of the participants in Vignette 2, to more deeply
understand how racism permeates through settler national identity.
Synthesizing the participant conversations through a character in this
monologue is an example of using a narrative form to summarize what
has been learned. In *How Societies Remember*, the argument is made for
how the narratives we hear about the past help to create the realities we
experience in the present day (Connerton, 1989, p. 2). As highlighted
in *I'm Still Canadian, Dad!*, the images and narratives of what it means to
"be Canadian" for a white settler have been ingrained through (among
other things) commercials for beer ads. These shared understandings
of the past then become social memories and are performed through
stories that are shared. The "collection of all stories we've inherited from
those that have come before" are our "narrative inheritance" (Ballard &
Ballard, 2011, p. 73). Fitzpatrick (2018) argues that the non-Indigenous

person must remember these stories in order to then tell alternative his/her/theirstories and knowledges, along with the political and social conditions that contributed to the processes of colonization.

Narratives in this chapter are categorized and discussed according to the initial themes of appropriation and embodiment, and centring the self within a community. These themes emerged as a part of the first fine-grained analysis of the research data when considering how to answer the research question: *What dispositions do pre- and in-service teachers need to develop in order to enact critical-creative agency through the lived provincial arts curriculum?* and when considering the two goals of this research:

- To empower teachers to use the arts to teach social justice curriculum
- To understand phenomenological bracketing through play-building

Appropriation and Embodiment

Cultural appropriation, or the adoption of elements of a culture or identity by someone from another culture or identity, is extremely problematic when someone from a dominant group appropriates food, clothing, music, art, and so on from a minority group. In the art world, conversations around appropriation have given rise to important ethical, aesthetic, and identity-related questions, such as whether cultural appropriation can give rise to aesthetically successful works of art (Young, 2010) and whether stronger copyright laws can be created to ensure that Aboriginal identity, represented through art, is recognized as collective ownership in perpetuity. (Coleman, 2005). In drama and theatre education, concerns around appropriation and the embodiment process are complicated when the actor has to physically, mentally, and emotionally create and then perform a character. Working with pre- and in-service teacher-actors can be additionally challenging if participants are performing for the first time, because in classrooms, the teacher's body is either highly *visible* (i.e., as clearly marked by ethnicity, race, size, disability, gender, sexuality, pregnancy, class, age or a combination of these or other attributes) or *invisible* (i.e., fitting into a student's preconceived idea of what a teacher's body should look like – white, female, heterosexual, middle class) (Freedman et al., 2003). Not surprisingly, the participants across the vignettes exhibited a spectrum of recognition related to this theme. Some participants, such as Astrid in Vignette 1, were highly attuned to issues of appropriation and embodiment, while others, such as the actors in *Sing the Brave Song: This Isn't Over!*, learned, researched, and discussed appropriation as a part of the rehearsal process. Examples from each vignette are presented below to illustrate how participants conceived of and worked through tensions related to appropriation and embodiment during play-building processes.

Vignette 1: Astrid

> At the beginning of the KAIROS activity I had this overwhelming feeling that "this is not my story." I really resisted playing a role that I realized probably comes from some common and current discourses on appropriation … and I didn't want to do something that could be hurtful to others … but then this initial feeling gave way to something else … a feeling that this particular story and activity was a story of welcoming. There is a palpable difference between appropriation and embodiment. Appropriation is a kind of theft, where Aboriginal stories, cultural practices and ideas are taken up, and used, and profited on by colonizers. Embodiment on the other hand, is what was happening in this exercise. This particular opportunity was created and written by those who have been oppressed and they have invited me into a role to understand … (Astrid, interview transcript, 2016)

Astrid's reflections on being a part of the KAIROS Blanket Exercise that asked her to take on the role of an Aboriginal person inform current conversations and concerns related to appropriation vs. appreciation and drama education. Linking performance to appropriation is a difficult conversation because the nature of drama and theatre in Western traditions holds fast to the notion that when we act and take on a character, we are essentially stepping into the life, mannerisms, mind frame, experiences, attitudes, and feelings of the character we are portraying. The actor must also consider the context of the larger story being told, and bear in mind the notes of the director and playwright. The actor has some autonomy in the way that they bring this character to life, but there are limits.

Astrid's concerns related to appropriation and embodiment during her participation in the KAIROS Blanket Exercise led me to ask her to speak to this tension during her interview. She said: "Appropriation is a kind of theft, where Aboriginal stories, cultural practices, and ideas are taken up, and used, and profited on by colonizers. Embodiment, on the other hand, is what was happening in this exercise because we were invited to learn about a more complete version of Canadian history, and this was shared with us." Astrid's comments are significant because she is including "embodiment," and "intentionality," in this conversation. If concerns around appropriation in art are in part linked to a collective cultural identity or misrepresentation of ceremonies, stories, and histories for the purposes of colonization (Coleman, 2005), then the guideposts she names "embodiment," and "intentionality," may help frame a conversation around ethics and responsibility when thinking about what stories are told and by whom. In relation to the objectives of this research, Astrid also articulates a discomfort in "bracketing the subjective self" when taking on a role in the KAIROS Blanket Exercise as she describes how she "really resisted playing a role that [she] realized probably comes from some common and current discourses on appropriation [because she] didn't want to do something that could be hurtful to others."

Vignette 2: Rewriting and Props

Appropriation and embodiment were also significant concerns for the cast of *Sing the Brave Song: This Isn't Over!* and Alayna Kolodziechuk, the playwright and director. Alayna, a white, cis-gender, able-bodied female, in her late twenties from Atlantic Canada, holds an undergraduate degree in history and philosophy with an emphasis on human rights, and a law degree. She wrote the play because she "was inspired by the reconciliation process that we are all tasked to find our role in ... and [she] really wanted to do what [she] could as far as the script and as a director were concerned, to recognize First Nations people's contributions to Canada." Initially, the creation of this play was intended to be an exploration around what could be learned by mounting a production based on the research findings from Vignette 1 with pre-service teachers. However, the pre-service education students who participated in Vignette 1 were not available to perform in the show, because the (free) on-campus theatre space booked for this play was only available after classes finished in the summer semester. This meant that most undergraduate students from the drama education course were no longer on campus, and that an open casting call that sought to recruit a diverse group of actors had to be posted. To recruit participants on a volunteer basis, a variety of strategies were used. First, the playwright, producer, and stage manager posted ads for the recruitment of actors on social media sites and in public areas in downtown Montreal, as well as sending ads to colleagues in theatre education programs at other institutions. Allan Vicaire at First Peoples' House also sent out a call to help recruit Indigenous performers from the local community. After a month, Allan reported back that the interested Indigenous actors were a part of a professional association, and so they would not be able to perform on the campus stage. If we could secure a professional stage, they could participate, but they would also require equity wages. As a devised theatre piece, originally intended to include student-actors, this was not possible because there was no budget to pay actors or rent a professional stage for rehearsals and performances. Thus, a play written for a diverse group of actors existed, but after two months of open casting, the four interested volunteer actors were:

Julie, a settler descent, cis-gender, able-bodied, female in her early 20s from Quebec, Canada, and an actor just finishing her BEd degree at McGill University. Julie heard about the play through my open invitation at the end of her Winter 2017 Curriculum and Instruction in Drama education course and wanted to learn more about Canadian Indigenous topics.

Julianna, settler descent, cis-gender, able-bodied, female in her 20s from Quebec, Canada, and an actor with a BA from McGill in psychology. At the time of the production, Julianna worked at McGill in student services and heard about the project through Julie, who encouraged her to audition because she was looking for acting opportunities.

Jesse, settler descent, able-bodied, male in his 20s from British Columbia, Canada, who brought his background in theatre (BFA) from Simon Fraser University to his role as an actor. At the time of the performance, he was a MA in Teaching and Learning student at McGill. Jesse's initial interest for participating in the project was a result of his own reflections on how "to think of ways to incorporate theatre into my teaching practices."

Asha, settler descent, cis-gender, able-bodied female, in her late teens from Alaska, USA.

An actor and dancer in the show, at the time of the performance she had just completed the first year of an Arts undergrad degree at McGill. Asha was interested in acting when she saw the call on her theatre faculty listserv.

Because of the challenges with casting, cancelling the show or rewriting the script were discussed. These two options seemed to be the only plausible ones at the time given financial and time constraints. The subsequent devised process centred on the conversations and topics that emerged during rehearsals, as articulated by Julianna:

> We had a lot of discussions about it, and I think Alayna really wanted us to feel comfortable and wanted us to understand it was no one's goal to be appropriative or speak for somebody else. I think that in the script, maybe initially, there were parts for Indigenous cast members, but those were reworked so that we would feel comfortable with presenting dialogue on important issues but not to speak for people with other positionalities than we had. Yeah, we had a lot of conversations, and then we'd read through how these conversations were reflected in script changes. (Julianna, interview transcript, 2017)

Once the revised script was completed, it was shared with Ethel Stevenson, who provided the research team with her feedback and thoughts on the content and direction of the production. Some of her specific recommendations were to change the terms used in the play to reflect "the shifts in governmental policy that have been used to identify Indigenous peoples from Indians to Natives to Aboriginals to Indigenous" and to also include specific information such as "suicide rates, the Indian Act, concerns related to assimilation, colonization, the introduction of alcohol to some Native communities, the fur trade and youth & prescription pills." Considering the historical significance of the terms used by the government to identify Indigenous people, this note offered an opportunity to more deeply understand the issues being explored and how assimilation and colonization policies impact current realities. Ethel also reminded the cast that "stories can be good medicine too" (Justice, 2018). This feedback became a part of the following scene:

SCENE 12: PEGGY FORMSMA

> [Asha enters stage left.]

ASHA: Earlier this year, Peggy Formsma of Attawapiskat said: "People portray the negative stuff, what about the beauty? What about the resilience? What we came through? We're still here. We're still here. And we are a strong people."

> [Asha exits stage left.]

The inclusion of this short scene, in which there is a focus on remembering the importance of resiliency and beauty, was an important reminder for how stories can also "drive out the poison and heal the spirit as well as the body" (Justice, 2018). This message of hope was further articulated in an audience comment responding to Scene 6, where Asha used dance to represent and remember the missing and murdered Indigenous women and girls (MMIWG) in Canada. In this scene, Asha dances with a red dress and then grieves as she realizes that the wearer of the dress will not return home. After the completion of this dance, the other actors mindfully placed red dresses on undetectable hooks throughout the intimate black box theatre space. The use of the red dress can be viewed as an example of how objects have agency of their own. An audience member commented:

> I guess, for me, one of the most moving parts of the play – and now that we're talking about appropriation, I think – was when you took the dresses

and hung them around, and when you passed out the posters. Because to me, you didn't speak for someone else or appropriate anything, you used the posters (of the missing women) and red dresses to make the audience feel like these women were with us. So, even though they weren't physically present, I thought of them as if they were standing here, as if there were Indigenous women here. So, I feel like that was a really great way of bringing in at least the women who'd gone missing and who don't have voices. I did feel like that was a respectful way of having them here and opening up awareness about this issue for people who may not know about this situation.

It's important to not just learn the facts about these issues but to feel them. The emotion of the situations you presented – like the woman losing her daughter in the dance with the red dress – just lingers with you.

The potential problem that the first audience member speaks about is that the use of the red dresses could be interpreted as appropriative. This indicates that there is a strong connection between the use of objects and the stories they have the potential to tell. In this instance, audience feedback indicates that the red dresses represented the missing women in a respectful way. However, when putting together a production such as this, ensuring that a sufficient amount of time is given to dialoguing about the meaning behind the use of certain objects, texts, or ideas is an important consideration because this impacts what the audience is ultimately able to take from the play. In this example, the cast of *Sing the Brave Song* spent time researching Jaime Black's original RE-Dress project (2014), reaching out to Black, a multidisciplinary artist of Anishinaabe and Finnish descent, to learn about the permanent exhibit of this project at the Canadian Museum of Human Rights, and speaking to the Faculty of Education's Artist in Residence, Lori Beavis, of Anishinaabe and Irish-Welsh descent, about how to appropriately include the red dresses in the production.

Additional conversations centred on agential realism and whether or not objects or stories ultimately have their own agency. Using the red dress as a metaphor that had shared meaning allowed for a collective experience in the dramatic space. If the phenomenological premise "what is important are not claims about reality, but how consciousness experiences the world" holds, then the audience viewing Asha dancing with a red dress can be interpreted as the subject and object not being separate from one another in the theatrical moment because the dress is intertwined with a direct experience in the world. This orientation "conceives of matter itself as lively or as exhibiting agency" (Coole & Frost, 2010, p. 9) and resists dualisms, binaries, and dialectical reconciliation

Image 3.1. Rehearsing for *Sing the Brave Song: This Isn't Over!* with red dresses placed against the backdrop. Photo taken by the author.

by espousing a "monological account of emergent, generative material being" (p. 8).

Thus, what could have been eliminated from the production (i.e., Asha's dance with the red dress), became an emotional spark that provoked audience engagement. In order to build on the emotional engagement created by this scene, the talkback sessions were used to provide a dialogical space for the audience to engage in deeper conversations. This process of feeling deeply and then moving our emotions to action is important. As Hayner reminds us: "We must remember what happened in order to keep it from happening again. But we must forget the feelings, the emotions that go with it. It is only by forgetting that we are able to go on" (2001, p. 1).

Julianna also reflected on the importance of shifting conversations because, she said, "It is easy to get stuck right now in discourses around appropriation but, we need to find ways of opening up spaces to move forward and not just shut things down." This comment reinforces how labelling something as "appropriative," while sometimes viable, can also prematurely end what could be productive learning. Julianna goes on to name some of the ways the cast and playwright were able to bring forward important content in a non-appropriative way:

> We have the throat singing music that we have; we have different multimedia pieces with the videos of people talking; we show that when we're using quotes, we're saying that we're quoting somebody, and we're saying the names of missing women. I think that that's important, and I think that that helps a lot of people. There is power in knowing names. And we're also sharing our own struggle with learning about all of these things as settlers who want to learn what it means to work in solidarity.

Vignette 3: Outlier?

> So, they went with the idea of a show about reconciliation, I think it was seventy-five per cent in favour of that show idea, and obviously I want it to happen this year because we have, like this partnership with you guys, and the kids knew that too, so that was another reason that they wanted to do it this year. And it is aligned with my teaching goals too. I think we spent the last couple of years learning about topics such as residential schools and the experiences of some Indigenous children that we send the shoe boxes to, and I think it's always good to raise awareness – learning is great – but putting your knowledge into action is more important. (Jennifer, interview transcript, February 2019)

Jennifer, an in-service music teacher in her thirties from New Brunswick, is the main participant in Vignette 3. In relation to appropriation and embodiment, her experiences leading grade 5 and 6 students as they wrote and performed the original musical *Reconciliation!* can be described as an outlier in comparison to the other vignettes because, as illustrated through the opening quote of this section, her focus was on taking pedagogical responsibility for redress as a settler teacher. The theme of appropriation did not come up in any observations of rehearsals, or in interviews with Jennifer. This was surprising since it was a large focus in both Vignette 1 and Vignette 2, leading me to broach a conversation around appropriation with Jennifer because "research tells us that [white teachers], are among the most recalcitrant of learners when it comes to social justice education (Cochran-Smith, 2000; Roman, 1993; Rosenberg, 1997; Sleeter & Grant, 1987) so much so that the term 'white teacher' has become virtually synonymous with resistance; resistance to acknowledging the significance of constructions of race to identity formation and of perceiving themselves as white and therefore implicated in systems of domination" (Byrne, 2006, as cited in Strong-Wilson, 2006, p. 115). In response to this query, Jennifer replied:

> I still remember the day in class when I heard about residential schools for the first time. I was in my thirties and working on my MA in Education at McGill after having previously completed my BEd. Even though I had been teaching in Quebec for some time and grew up in New Brunswick, I had never heard of Indian Residential Schools. But the moment that I did I promised myself that I would never have a student who came through my classroom who did not learn about this part of Canadian history. So, I literally went home that night and I started googling and reading all about Indian residential schools and went into my own class the next day and told my class: "I never knew this when I was your age, but we're going to start learning together." So, from that day on I found ways to bring Indigenous content into the music curriculum through songs or stories or guest speakers.

Although she doesn't speak explicitly about appropriation, Jennifer's response addresses the research question that asks how a teacher can develop a disposition of critical and creative agency that enables them to find ways for including reconciliation in their work. Jennifer describes how she had already worked on the two important points that Astrid raised – "embodiment" and "intentionality" – and went further by bringing in IRS survivors to speak to her students. Further, Jennifer took up this work by changing her teaching practice when she learned about IRSs by including content by Indigenous musicians, authors, and artists ("I have the students read some Canadian literature stories like *I'm Not a Number* and *Stolen Words*") into the curriculum. Jennifer's experience illustrates that when an in-service teacher has arts training and the personal agency to include the Calls to Action for Education in the TRC in their teaching, they can find immediate ways to share this information with their students. However, having the personal impetus to do something is not always enough when dominant structures and long-held beliefs are being contradicted or challenged. To understand how Jennifer's agency as an educator was supported, we should consider it in relation to centring oneself within a community of practice.

Circles within Circles: Centring Oneself within a Community

> Foucault wrote about what he called political spirituality. This occurs he says, when people willfully – meaning "with alertness to the creative dimensions of their project" – seek a new way to establish a regime of truth and a regime of self-governance, each by and through the other. It is putting into

question one's style of existence and a process of founding, un-founding, re-founding, creating beginnings. (Ball, 2017, p. xii)

I think the most important thing is to have *community support*. So, obviously talking to your administration first, and talking to, also, your [cycle] teachers that are the kids that are doing the show is very important and giving people some background. It takes a *team*. (Jennifer, interview transcript, emphasis added, February 2019)

A community of practice (CoP) is a group of people "who share a concern or a passion for something they do and learn how to do it better as they interact regularly" (Wenger, 2000). CoPs come in different forms and sizes, they serve a variety of purposes, and they revolve around authentic tasks (Carter et al., 2020). The drama and theatre CoPs in the vignettes illustrate an example of an authentic opportunity for participants to work together in a supported environment to explore new pedagogical paradigms through embodiment and critical/creative discourse. If "the body is the inscribed surface of educational effects and it bears and manifests the effects of regulating discourses" (Foucault, 1984, p. 82), then feeling socio-emotionally engaged and moving one's body in new ways through the creation of characters to explore new narratives of power and truth offer opportunities to co-create new beginnings.

In the research notes, there were over fifty labels related to the categorization of critical self-reflection. Within these labels were categories that included self-awareness, pedagogical reflection, and risk. Risk emerged as the most frequent code within these categories, in relation to fostering creativity as a necessary condition for engaging in artistic processes. Generally, taking a risk in the drama education context can mean anything from leading a new warm-up activity you have never tried before to explaining what your interpretation of a performance is. Risk in the context of this research is related to an individual's self-expression of their engagement with understanding the TRC's Calls to Action for Education through drama and theatre. Centring oneself within a dialogic community can also be understood as spending time with one's own subjective experiences (as related to consciousness) when creating a character and working towards understanding the educational Calls to Action in the TRC. Engaging intersubjectively (during rehearsals) is then possible, as illustrated through the dialogue in Vignette 1.

Vignette 1: Reconciliation in Teacher Education

In Chapter 1 of *Reconceptualizing Teacher Education: A Canadian Contribution to a Global Challenge* (Phelan et al., 2020) Jan Hare describes how a shift in Indigenous-settler relations in Canada can take place through the preparation of settler pre-service teachers using a reconciliation framework. This framework includes three themes: how pre-service teachers make sense of reconciliation; the significance of residential school history as a necessary part of the curriculum and the role of teacher educators in addressing Indigenous perspectives; and content and pedagogies in the work of teacher educators with pre-service teachers (Hare, 2020, p. 29). She goes on to say that in educational contexts, reconciliation needs to be a part of dialogues that make up policies, programs, and practices in order to ensure that Call to Action no. 63 (pre-service teachers need to learn about the history and legacy of residential schools) occurs. In Vignette 1, Hare's framework and its three themes are illustrated through the work of students/participants in the curriculum and instruction in drama education course I taught at McGill in 2015–16. As a component of helping pre-service teachers learn about residential schools, make sense of reconciliation, and understand their responsibilities for redress, I considered my role as their instructor because the authority of a person teaching Indigenous perspectives and content is sometimes contested. This led me to ask Allan to collaborate. It was important for me to work with Allan on bringing conversations around reconciliation into the teacher education curriculum because there was no required course on Indigenous Education for pre-service teachers in their BEd at the time, and I wanted to make sure that students would be prepared to take up the Calls to Action of the TRC as in-service teachers when the time came.

While learning to become an ally scholar and teacher presents challenges and opportunities related to identity and authenticity, it can be far more difficult for Indigenous faculty members or in-service teachers to always be the ones to teach Indigenous courses (Hare, 2020, p. 37). Thus, working with Allan and then focusing on the importance of community in the drama education classroom were intentional and essential first steps for building a capacity for dialogue and learning with students. Co-creating the learning space through the simple ritual of taking off our shoes before entering the class and then sitting in a circle together to check in are just some of the ways that community was fostered from the first day of class. Using theatre strategies such as Forum Theatre also helped to facilitate a sense of collective belonging, as illustrated in the re-storied narrative dialogue below:

MINDY: Good-morning class. I can't believe we are almost halfway through the term already and that we are at the "Forum Theatre" segment of our course. As you probably noticed from the readings, Forum Theatre is a concept

that Augusto Boal coined when working with a troupe of
actors in Brazil who went into communities to work with
local people to explore some of the issues confronting
them in the present moment. He was a contemporary of
Freire, who I am sure many of you have heard of. Let's
see by a quick show of hands who knows a bit about
Freire's work. Great! Heidi, why don't you tell us a little
bit more.

HEIDI: Well, Paulo Freire was an educator and activist who encouraged illiterate people to become literate so that they
could learn to read their worlds literally and figuratively.
He thought that becoming educated was a process of
conscientization or developing a critical lens through
which to see one's life and place oneself within a larger
landscape.

MINDY: Wonderful, thanks! That was a really comprehensive and
succinct overview. I also particularly like his ideas around
critical pedagogies of hope, where he suggests that in any
struggle towards freedom or transformation, we need to
keep hope alive, so that education is not just about what
he calls the banking method, of depositing knowledge
into someone else's head, but is about helping them to
develop a critical reflection to action cycle around what
is learned. Does anyone else have something to add?
[Pause.] No? Ok, well, Boal worked alongside these educational ideas within a theatre context. So, rather than
audiences just being passive observers at the theatre, he
wanted to find ways to engage and activate them – he
even called his audiences "spect-actors." I was able to
study some of these techniques with Theatre of the Oppressed NYC and am really looking forward to leading
you through some of the basic ideas today. So, what we
are going to do during today's class is to engage in a
Forum Theatre-like activity. Some of you will start off as
performers in a scene where it will be up to you to suggest a real-world problem that you have recently been
confronted with and are still grappling with. Something
that happened but that has no solution. So, let's start with
this. Who has an idea for a problem we can all explore?

CLASSMATE 1:   How about what to do as a teacher on the school yard trying to break-up a fight?

MINDY:	Possibly. Let's hear everyone's ideas and then you can all vote on which one to explore. How does that sound?
	[Heads nod.]
	Okay.
CLASSMATE 2:	What about if a student tells you that they are cutting themselves, or suicidal?
CLASSMATE 3:	Sorry to lighten the mood, but how about the problem of like your online photo or presence? I know it sounds silly, but the pictures I have up of being on a beach vacation or whatever might not be good if I am applying for jobs soon.
MINDY:	All of these are great suggestions! Is the class ready to vote on which one you want to explore, or are there any last potential topics?
CLASSMATE 4:	[Hesitantly raising her hand.]
	Last night on my metro ride home two guys followed me after my stop and started calling me names because of my headscarf. I didn't know what to do. They said things like: "Paki, go home" and "Take that rag off your head, you're in Canada now." I was terrified and dropped my bag. I reached to pick it up and they came closer. I could feel my heart beating in my chest and bit my lip to fight off the tears. I said, "I was born here in Montreal, please leave me alone." I was thinking – how could this happen to me? I am a university student. I have never even travelled outside of Canada. And then a car drove nearby, and they ran off laughing. What if that car hadn't come?
MINDY:	I am sorry you had to experience that. But thank you for your bravery in sharing your story with the class.
	[Pause.]
	Okay, now, it looks like we have several options. To recap, our choices are how to intervene as a teacher in a school yard fight, how to respond to a suicidal student who discloses to you, the impact of one's social media presence on professionalism, and racist events on the metro. That gives us four options. I will number off one, two, three, and four. Please raise your hand to vote for one of the four topics to explore for this forum. We can close our eyes for this vote and then when the tabulation is finished I will share the results.

[Mindy calls out each number one to four and silently notes the number of votes for each option.]

Thank you! Please open your eyes. So, based on the class vote, the topic that we are going to explore for today's forum is number four. This was the situation in which Classmate 4 experienced a racist incident on the metro because of her hijab.

MINDY: [turns to Classmate 4 and asks her]

Would you be ok retelling your story?

CLASSMATE 4: [Nods.]

MINDY: Okay. In addition to yourself, what other characters do you need in this scene, if you are going to replay it exactly as you just told it?

CLASSMATE 4: The two people who followed me, maybe some passersby and the car driver.

MINDY: Perfect. Can I have people volunteer for each of these roles?

[Hands go up and students go onstage to represent each character.]

Now, before we start from the top with re-enacting the scene Classmate 4 just told us, there is one more thing about Forum Theatre I am going to add. The Joker. The Joker in Forum Theatre is someone who can stop and start a scene in order to try and get more of the audience involvement, or to try and get to the heart of what some of the onstage actors are thinking about. For Boal, he would start a scene with a real word issue and have his acting troupe play it through to the climax of the unresolved problem. Then the Joker would ask the spect-actors if any of them had ideas about how one of the characters could have done something differently to change the ending of the situation. So, in this case, the climax of the scene, or where we don't know what is going to happen next. When was that moment in Classmate 4's story?

CLASSMATE 5: Maybe when Classmate 4 dropped her bag and the men started walking closer.

MINDY: Sure. So, let's play the scene to that point and then if any of the audience members want to jump in with a different ending they will come up on stage and the actors on stage will improvise with them to create a new ending. Please also remember that people playing roles are always offering

their interpretations and they do not necessarily share the
beliefs and values of the characters they portray. Oh! And I
also want to make sure that we come back to a larger conversation about how we, as educators, address some of the
topics/issues that you all suggested for this forum (i.e., addressing trauma, racist incidents, and self-harm) during our
debrief. This conversation, as well as considering the ethics
of telling our own stories and those of others, are important
for us to check in about in relation to their personal and
pedagogical intersections and implications. Okay, any questions? No? Okay, for now I will play the Joker. Don't forget
to call curtain to start and end the scene.

The adapted forum work continued, and students slowly got the hang
of stepping in to replace their classmates in the scene to explore alternative endings to the problem presented. Conversations around what
worked or could be changed after new ideas were presented kept pop-
ping up, leading to offshoots of ideas throughout the room. After the
activity concluded, Teresa, a participant, shared her thoughts on this
activity: "I found this activity to be very eye opening. It has offered me
the shared perspectives of other students confronting racism. The conversations about this made me think about being on practicum and how
I always get approached by teachers and asked to teach about Aboriginal
topics. These requests are in schools outside my community, and in it.
Oftentimes I find myself sugar-coating the historical facts that I am always asked to share on practicum about what happened to Aboriginal
people in Canada because I don't want to offend anyone."
    In this comment, Teresa shares her experiences around how she
teaches Aboriginal issues to non-Aboriginal students and teachers on
her practicum: by sugar-coating them. She talks about not wanting to offend others, and thus glosses over historical events. Observing the Forum
Theatre activity about another student's lived experience opened up a
space for Teresa to share a bit about how the IRS experience affected her
family and to connect the two experiences to examples of racism.
    This realization ultimately led Teresa to co-create a final performance
piece in which she and three other students, including Astrid, chose to
turn the classroom space into the Montreal metro where each of the students in her group got on the train and stood with a backpack. The rest of
the class sat in chairs facing inwards beside the actors and together rode
the metro to McGill station. One by one the performers stood up and
opened their backpacks. As items were removed, the objects became provocations that told the story of the "baggage" that they carried around with
them. This example of using an object to illicit a story led to the sharing

of unique stories and experiences. Teresa chose to focus her monologue on some of her own experiences with systemic racism as a Mohawk woman and the intergenerational traumas that she had lived through. This was difficult, to say the least, and part way through her monologue she had to stop because it was too hard for her to finish. Instead, she handed her story to a classmate and asked them to pick up where she had left off. Her classmates paused in silence when the monologue ended. They gave her story space and honour and then several of them embraced her with a hug.

As Marjorie Beaucage, Metis, reminds us: there are "different kinds of medicine" that different people need in order to change and grow. Teresa's story led to a frank conversation about not only her experiences, but those of others in the class. Her story opened up a place of healing for her and for her classmates because "stories and tears are medicine" (Beaucage, 2019). That day we all learned that if we take the time to think a little more about those around us and get to know one another a bit more, we can see that we all have stories that are difficult and painful, that we all need to show ourselves and one another a little bit more kindness and compassion because all human beings experience pain, hurt, and suffering. But sharing our stories can also teach us to grow in new and unexpected ways and that sometimes we need the help of other people that we trust to help us tell our truths.

Vignette 2: Meta-Narratives and Education

The scene "We start here" was written *to reflect* the actual conversations that emerged from the actors in *Sing the Brave Song: This Isn't Over!* when Alayna asked them what they knew about the TRC's educational Calls to Action. The TRC, as previously described, was tasked with uncovering the truth about what happened during the residential school period in Canada. After collecting more than 7,000 statements from school survivors, the TRC made ninety-four Calls to Action to address the legacy of the residential schools and reconcile the broken relationship between Indigenous and non-Indigenous Canadians. Overall, the actors felt that they had a partial understanding of Canadian Indigenous history for two reasons. First, there was a lack of knowledge about Indigenous "history pre- and post-contact." These "gaps between historical and contemporary realities of colonialism" were linked to contemporary systemic issues of colonialism and race. Because of the specific lens that the actors saw the world through before coming to this work, they grappled with learning some really hard truths about the actual reality being lived by many Aboriginal people, and so, to engage with the learning process necessary to co-create the final production, they began by looking at their own history and experiences. In this way starting "here" meant asking: What do I personally know about the TRC? What do I need to know? Starting with the self in relation to exploring the TRC and supplementary texts also led to conversations about anti-oppression, social justice, and white privilege. As a part of the play-creation process, Allan said that all pre- and in-service teachers should be learning and teaching about the TRC in their classrooms: "If you do your research and you do your work, you definitely have to teach about the TRC ... It's not like saying, I'm not gonna do it because I'm not Indigenous. So, that's the message that needs to come across. Yes, you can do your research, invite Elders, speak to them, research, bring in people who can start a conversation with you."

SCENE 3: WE START HERE

[Jesse enters at stage right; Julianna enters at stage left.]

JESSE: Indigenous students in Canada have the highest drop-out, absenteeism, and adolescent suicide rates in the country.

JULIANNA: Many teacher education programs are investing heavily in resources and initiatives on Indigenous topics. However, most Quebec institutions have not to the same extent.

Part of this project is to bring Quebec Indigenous content and related issues of equity and diversity into the teacher education program at McGill using drama and theatre.

[Acknowledge each other.]

JESSE: In considering the issues facing Indigenous peoples in education, the impact of Canada's Indian Residential School system can't be ignored.

As a result of the residential schools, the educational experience of Indigenous children has been defined by policies intended to create long-lasting damage. Abuse and neglect of children in the schools was rampant, education poor.

Consider S. R. McVitty, principal of Mount Elgin Industrial School, who said: "In the case of the Indian, a little learning is a dangerous thing."

JULIANNA: The purpose of the residential schools, it was said, was "to kill the Indian in the child."

JESSE: Canada's Truth and Reconciliation Commission was tasked with uncovering the truth about what happened during the residential school period. After collecting more than 7,000 statements from school survivors, the Commission made ninety-four Calls to Action to address the legacy

of the residential schools and reconcile the broken
relationship between Indigenous and non-Indigenous
Canadians.

JULIANNA: The Commission says, "reconciliation is not an Aboriginal
problem, it is a Canadian one."
We start here.
[Both step forward.]

To discuss the TRC and create the scene above, Alayna brought in the
TRC's executive summary, the TRC's educational Calls to Action, and
justice and news items that were available at the time. To engage with
these texts, she used the prompt: What do these articles say and not say?
For Jesse, this was an important way to start a conversation around what
content should be prioritized. He felt that "this experience gave us all
a chance to read some direct testimonies of for example, Indian Residential School survivors, and then to talk about what it means to take
up some of the Calls to Action in the TRC." The opportunity to look at
direct testimonies and talk about them was not something that any of
the cast members had had the opportunity to do prior to this process.
The rehearsal process began with the gaps in information that the participants had but led to an opportunity for individuals to "do the work"
that Allan says is required of settlers and newcomers in order to engage
in the calls of the TRC. Participants described how "doing the work" is a
personal and collaborative undertaking. To centre the self, participants
identified the following steps that they went through as a part of their
experience of preparing to perform in *Sing the Brave Song: This Isn't Over!*:

1 Start with a personal exploration of one's own positionality and privi-
lege(s) or barriers experienced;
2 Be open to learning more about something you may only have a general knowledge of;
3 Be prepared to individually and collectively explore the topic/issue
through available texts (through reading, conversation, and embodied explorations vis-à-vis the TRC, books, news articles, survivor testimonies); and
4 Actively work to co-create learning opportunities around the topics/
issues that individuals and the group need to learn about/explore.

As a result of the collaborative play-creation process, and represented in the final scene of the play, the cast shared that their discussions and experiences working on the play helped them to understand

that reconciliation is a relational action, which they described in the following ways:

1 Starts with a land acknowledgement that goes beyond a generic one created by an institution: *We recognize that we are gathered today on the traditional territory of the Kanien'kehá:ka people, and that this land is subject to the Two Row Wampum Treaty.*
2 Requires one to ask and answer for yourself what "reconciliation" means: Acceptance. Understanding. Knowing the truth. Building trust. Being brave and acknowledging that reconciliation has to be something we all commit to as Canadians.
3 Requires listening.
4 Acknowledges that any reconciliation with the Indigenous people in Canada will have to include reconciliation with the environment.
5 Puts pressure on our government to honour the treaties and call for the full implementation of the *United Nations Declaration on the Rights of Indigenous Peoples.*
6 Requires reading some of the 556 memoirs and anthologies by residential school survivors that have been published.
7 Celebrates how Aboriginal people have maintained their identity and their communities despite being subjected to aggressive assimilation policies for nearly 200 years.
8 Means buying from First Nations businesses. Supporting Indigenous artists. Making art together.
9 Reminds us not to be afraid to question things. Notice things. Being aware of the impact of the words we use.
10 Is about being mindful. Being respectful and continuing this work.

The processes and strategies that Alayna, Asha, Jesse, Julianna, and Julie engaged in to co-create *Sing the Brave Song* are specific play-building strategies that Weigler (2001) describes in *Strategies for Playbuilding* and which can be used as a valuable starting point for this work in one's own classroom. In this book, recalling stories and unpacking them, weaving individual performance pieces into a show, and beginning with a group's questions are proven approaches to help a group translate issues into theatre. Approaches such as these, and others, were also used by Jennifer and her grade 5 and 6 students in the creation of *Reconciliation!*

Vignette 3: Circles within Circles

Just to go back to that first day with my students, I just told them "I don't know enough about this, so we're going to learn together." I think being able to start from that place of vulnerability is really important. But, as a settler, I do have this lack of knowledge about Indigenous peoples, due to a longstanding lack of education in our country. So yeah, the vulnerable position a settler must be willing to be in to know how easily misrepresentation and false information can occur in this context, even when one is actively teaching about Indigenous history and reconciliation, is real. So, I have had to come to terms with making mistakes during this process, totally unintentionally, but I shared them with my students, so that they would know that everyone can make mistakes and then grow from them too. (Jennifer, interview transcript, February 2019)

Jennifer describes a similar process to the four steps identified by the cast in *Sing the Brave Song: This Isn't Over!* when "doing the work." She describes having to admit what you don't know, being able to dwell in a vulnerable position that will allow you to learn from/with others, and to be ready to take risks and learn from your mistakes. This description speaks to the overarching research question in this book in that it contemplates what ethos teachers need to embody in order to take up critical and creative issues in their classrooms. It is only after this initial positioning that, in Jennifer's case, she sought buy-in from her students. "So, after asking my students if they wanted to work on this topic, and they did, we did! So, buy-in was really important, and I just never would have started this whole undertaking if the students didn't also want to focus on the creation of this piece." Checking in with her students demonstrates a commitment to relational learning and community. This also exemplifies the ripple effect from the "start with the smallest circles first" teaching because after she checked in with her students about working on this play and had their support, she immediately reached out for administrative and parental support, which she indicates "was an important step because co-creating an original musical is a deviation from the regular shows that I've had at the school (i.e., using pre-written musicals written for elementary schools). And you know, they are all pretty 'fun' and 'light-hearted.'" Jennifer also shows foresight by making sure that she had the principal's support, first and foremost. When speaking with the principal, Jennifer learned that the principal actually didn't know about residential schools herself, and so this was another opportunity to experience how working within a school to learn about the TRC can have immediate impact on the school community.

In addition to reaching out to administration, other teachers and parents, Jennifer also began collaborating with Tom, Lisa, Nina, Barbara, and the research team (Mindy and two research assistants). This support helped Jennifer confront some of the "negative reactions of parents, who may not want these difficult issues of social justice discussed with

Image 3.2. The KAIROS and McGill research team who worked with Jennifer and her students. Photo taken by Linda Handiak.

their young children." Because of the potential for parental concern about the play, "the trust of administration, students and families in the school was important because many parents did not know about various aspects of Indigenous history in Canada and moving the conversation from the classroom to the home was important for me." The ripple effect of this production was strong, and the school-community-university partnership overlapped to support not only the creation of the production but helped to hold the work of the students, who had been learning about IRSs and the experiences of students their age in Attawapiskat and Kangiqsualujjuaq throughout their elementary education.

As Jennifer describes, the creation of the play is an "action [taken] together, to understand, to deal with the given problem that we share in

common (i.e., Calls to Action in the TRC) [because alone none] of us
has the knowledge that's required to solve that problem. The knowledge
itself is the product of our action" (O'Neal, as cited in Hammer, 1992,
p. 139). Jennifer continues:

> In this instance, the action [of creating and performing *Reconciliation!*] led
> to the regional director of the Lester B. Pearson School Board approach-
> ing me and my principal. They asked if they could bus in all of the grade
> 5 students from the school board to watch this show. So, of course the stu-
> dents were asked if they would like to put on a second performance of their
> production, and they agreed that they would like to share this with other
> students. The bussing of students and my substitution costs for the day
> were covered, and so it's kind of a tangible outcome that can be viewed as
> an indicator that the undertaking had impact and value, beyond what was
> anticipated during the conception period. (Jennifer, interview transcript,
> February 2019)

Jennifer and her students' experience of co-creating and performing
Reconciliation! was a commitment in and through time to take action together on a social justice issue. Their knowledge and the ultimate sharing of this engagement through theatre was a gift for their audience. "It
takes seven generations for things to change" is a teaching that rang out
at the conclusion of the play on 27 March 2019, as a grandparent at the
end of the production stood up and said: "I lived in a community where
residential schools were seen as an essential and positive nation building
activity. My parents told me this, I believed it and supported this idea. Tonight, my grandson has taught me something new ... all of you children
have ... A new story about the impact of this legacy."

This vignette focuses on the experiences of Jennifer, as a Quebec
teacher who illustrates how if one is passionate about social justice, one
can use the arts curriculum to teach students about a variety of related
topics and issues. This case study speaks directly to the overarching question in this book about whether or not the Quebec arts curriculum can
allow for teacher agency to flourish within a school environment and
to ultimately impact the related community of teachers, staff, students,
and parents. The focus of this vignette is on the significance of the relationships and community support that Jennifer was able to establish in
order to develop *Reconciliation!* and her ability to "reach in" to her own
concern about learning more about Indigenous topics in order to teach
her students. Jennifer's pedagogical wherewithal to connect this content
to the arts curriculum through music, drama, and theatre illustrates

how building relationships and fostering community are essential for an undertaking such as this because support is needed in order to tackle themes such as loss and residential schools with grades 5 and 6 students.

SCENE 4: LOSS (5NM)
Backstage: picture of first contact, cold northern scene, De Beers/ Attawapiskat on news, protests
Props: blanket
Actors: Six mains, two settlers (meant to be like Gaston/Lefou characters from Beauty and the Beast), two Indigenous people, one Indigenous Chief, two news reporters

KID 1:	That was really amazing! It reminds me of watching the Elders dance at the Powwow last summer.
ELDER 1:	Yes, we have such talent among our people. Our traditions of old are still alive and well today.
KID 2:	There is so much to celebrate: creation, Mother Earth, Sky Woman, Turtle Island, our songs, music and dance. Wow!
KID 4:	I must admit, that instrument and dance were pretty cool. Thinking I should jet soon though, so I have some iPad time!
KID 3:	All the stories so far have such happy endings. Do you have any stories that don't end so well?
KID 4:	Now that could be something interesting … maybe I'll stick around for a while.
ELDER 2:	Let me tell you about what happened to our land … [Spotlight pans to the top stage. Three Indigenous people off to side of stage talking in a circle. Two settlers approach.]
SETTLER 1:	Look at all of this beautiful land!
SETTLER 2:	Hey, wait! There's people here. Who are those people? [Settlers approach the group, Indigenous people turn toward them.]
SETTLER 1:	Hello. Do you live here?
SETTLER 2:	Yeah, yeah, do you live here? Is this your land?
CHIEF:	Whoa! Slow down. We live here, but the land is not ours. We belong to this land. Our ancestors have been here for thousands of years. We'd like to welcome you. Come over here, we'll show you how we live. [Spotlight pans to front of stage.]

ELDER 1:   When Europeans first came, they had much to learn. We taught them how to fish, hunt, and which plants were medicine, and which were poisonous.

ELDER 2:   We traded our furs and medicines for items like weapons and spices. Things seemed to be going well.......
UNTIL
[Spotlight pans to back stage where settlers are speaking in hushed tones.]

SETTLER 1:   We need to tell the King about all this land. We need to take control. This land shall be ours.

SETTLER 2:   Yes, yes, tell the king. Tell the king. This land SHALL be ours.

SETTLER 1:   Indeed. We need a plan. More of us, less of them.
[Spotlight pans to front stage.]

ELDER 1:   Slowly, over time, the Europeans took our land. We had less and less space and were forced from our homes.

KID 4:   That's awful. How?

ELDER 2:   Many of us were made to move far north, to a land we weren't familiar with. We weren't used to it, and treacherous winter conditions made it hard to survive.

ELDER 1:   Diseases like smallpox and tuberculosis were brought over from Europe.
Sometimes, these diseases were spread intentionally among our people.
[Spotlight pans to back of stage. Settler 1 coughing on blanket in the background. Three Indigenous people are off to the side talking.]

SETTLER 1:   We brought you some supplies.

INDIGENOUS 1: That is helpful. Thank you very much.

SETTLER 2:   [nudging Settler 1 discreetly]
Of course, that's right. These will definitely help.

INDIGENOUS 2: So many of our people are becoming sick.

SETTLER 1:   [Nudges back, coughs in blanket again, hands blankets to the Chief. Spotlight pans to the front of stage.]

KID 1:   Do you mean that these diseases were given to our people on purpose?

ELDER 2:   Sadly, yes, that happened in many cases.

KID 4:   Whoa, seriously?! That really is a terrible ending.

ELDER 1:	Over time, we worked to get along with the settlers. Treaties were signed between our people and the Crown. In these agreements, we agreed to share some of our ancestral land and resources in exchange for various payments and promises.
ELDER 2:	Our grandfathers and grandmothers signed these treaties, not just for themselves, but for seven generations ahead, including all of you. For our people, they were considered a sacred agreement between nations.
KID 3:	This sounds promising. Negotiating is always helpful for us kids at recess.
ELDER 1:	It did sound promising at the beginning. However, we've seen many situations where the treaties were forgotten as soon as money and valuable resources came into play. [Spotlight pans to the back of stage, where a news reporter is at a desk reporting.]
REPORTER 1:	Good evening folks. First tonight, we have another tragic story of Indigenous treaties being forgotten here in Canada. Recently, South African mining giant, De Beers, has decided to develop Ontario's first diamond mine in Attawapiskat.
REPORTER 2:	That's right _____(name), people living in the Attawapiskat First Nation have held many protests recently as their traditional hunting grounds are being dug up in search of diamonds.
REPORTER 1:	Yes _____, behind us you see a picture of one of those protests. De Beers arrived in Attawapiskat just after the news that their elementary school had been contaminated by 150,000 litres of diesel that had leaked into the substructure.
REPORTER 2:	A lack of clean drinking water and proper shelter plague the community where De Beers has set up shop. The challenges are many for these folks, that is for sure.

In addition to this scene, *Reconciliation!* focused on stories of resiliency, community, culture, and oral storytelling. These themes were equally important for the fifth and sixth grade students to learn about, so that they could understand what their own responsibilities working towards reconciliation could look like. In Scene 6, *Standing Up*, after learning about residential schools, Kid 4 says:

KID **4:**   That's terrible. Did anyone take responsibility or apologize
                    to our people?
                    [said angrily]

This line, indicates that students recognize that there needs to be redress
following the experiences of children in Canadian residential schools. In
response to this line, another actor says:

ELDER **1:**   Yes, after many years, the Government of Canada finally
                    apologized for residential schools. Sadly, an apology
                    does not erase the many wrongs that have been done.

The musical concludes soon thereafter with a reminder that "it is
through you, our youth, that real change can come. Your actions and
words can raise awareness and bring together people from all backgrounds." When these lines were spoken, the song *Dreamchild*, originally
created by students of St. Willibrord in Chateauguay, Quebec was sung
by the St. Edmund's students. *Dreamchild* combines English, French, and
Mohawk languages to convey a powerful message of unity, love, and respect. During the performances of *Reconciliation,* Nina also joined in by
interlaying her Inuit throat singing overtop the children's harmonious
voices.

Discussion

Jennifer literally began to find a way to teach her own students about
Indian Residential Schools hours after she learned about them for the
first time. This initial reaction and impulse echoes the belief of Paulette
Regan (2010) that education is not simply about the transfer of knowledge but is a transformative experiential learning that empowers people to make change in the world. In *Unsettling the Settler Within,* Regan
recounts her own personal journey engaging in Indigenous-settler relations as the director of research for the Truth and Reconciliation Commission of Canada, where she calls on "other non-Native Canadians to
take a critical look at how the history of the country is presented and
to open themselves up to the idea that violence lies at the core of relations between Euro-Canadians and Indigenous people" (Regan, 2010, as
cited in Hallam, 2011). Despite the reassurance by Regan that there is no
one-size-fits-all approach to reconciliation, Jennifer's story of just starting
where she was at (i.e., hearing about Indian Residential Schools, and
then researching as much as she could about the subject before sharing this information with her students honestly and openly) provides

an example of how we can all learn a bit more about this process and why it is a necessary undertaking. This was possible because of her own willingness to "plumb the depth of our repressed history, so that we can risk interacting differently with Indigenous peoples – with vulnerability, humility and a willingness to stay in the decolonizing struggle of our own discomfort" (Regan 2010). Articulated in slightly different terms, Strong-Wilson (2007) draws on Byrne (2006) to argue that there is a specific decolonization process of the "white" subject, one that

> is a different kind of project from the one Smith (1999) described, although it shares with it the goal of social change. Feminist theorists Smith and Watson (1992), in *De/Colonizing the Subject: The Politics of Gender in Women's Autobiography*, adopt Mohanty's definition of colonization as "a relation of structural domination, and a suppression – often violent – of the heterogeneity of the subject(s) in question" (Mohanty, as cited in Smith & Watson, p. xvi) and of decolonization as a set of "strategies" to address these "colonial practices" (p. xvi) via "the deformation/reformation of identity" (pp. xviii–xix). The deformation/reformation needs to happen to the "I" or "autobiographical subject" (p. xvii), one that, for white women, addresses hegemony and colonization. Decolonization of the white subject is thus best seen as a subset of a larger project of decolonization: "If a field of 'white studies' exists at all, it is at most a subset of other concerns around 'race' and identity." (Byrne, 2006, as cited in Strong-Wilson, 2007, p. 117)

Through Strong-Wilson's (2007) discussion of the decolonization of the white woman's deformation/reformation in relation to the "I" one can further understand Jennifer's impulse to begin with her own process of deformation/reformation and desire to do something different through her teaching as a result. Over time this engagement led to a reformation of her own identity as a teacher because she "gave her heart to" the ongoing work of reconciliation as a relational, pedagogical, and personal project.

The multiple connections that were made and strengthened as a result of the creation of *Reconciliation!* included teachers, administrators, parents, students, faculty, research assistants, Mohawk and Inuit Elders and artists, Mohawk teachers, school board administration, students from other schools, grandparents, and school staff.

This exemplifies how the "start with the smallest circles first" teaching can lead to larger changes, as long as collaboration, relational learning, and openness are a part of the process. In chapter 4, a series of connections across the vignettes is explored.

Chapter Four

Weaving Together Understandings across the Vignettes

Concepts are distilled images in any sensory form or combination of forms that are used to represent the particulars of experience. With concepts we can do two things that may very well be unique to our species: we can imagine possibilities we have not encountered, and we can try to create, in the public sphere, the new possibilities we have imagined in the private precincts of our consciousness. We can make the private public by sharing it with others. Transforming the private into the public is a primary process of work in both art and science. Helping the young learn how to make that transformation is another of education's most important aims.

E.W. Eisner, *The Arts and the Creation of Mind* (2002, p. 3)

The vignettes provide examples of how instructors, actors, students, and playwrights have used drama education and theatre to engage with concepts related to the ideas and aims of the TRC. These private/public engagements open spaces of learning, hope, and transformation for the participants, students, and audiences considering the topics presented in performance spaces. As discussed in chapter 3, initial vignette themes of appropriation, embodiment, and communities of practice emerged across studies. After considering these themes more deeply, new themes took shape: risk and learning as rupture, belonging, and unsettling/counter-narratives. At this time, each of the themes will be discussed in greater depth and then considered in relation to the emergent understandings.

Theme 1: Risk and Learning as Rupture

Defining Risk

The terms "risk" and "danger" seem out of place in an educational context because each of these words conjures up extreme possibilities of both bodily and psychological harm. At first, it seems unfathomable that in the context of education, where children and youth are placed in the proverbial hands of educators and schools to help prepare them to be contributing citizens of their respective societies, that there should ever be risks that lead to "dangerous" consequences.

However, taking risks emerged as a theme throughout the participants' experiences as they described and made sense of their engagements in drama education and theatre. This suggests that a different "reading" of risk could/should be considered when thinking about risk in art education contexts. For instance, both Arlene's comment about connection, "If I don't challenge myself to act, how can I expect my students to? I had to be brave and think about my students, instead of myself and I've never done that before," as well as Jennifer's motivation to create *Reconciliation!* to ensure that her students learned about a Canadian human rights issue that she had not learned about until completing her MA, illustrate how each woman took a risk as a way to improve as pedagogues. When one digs deeper into the literature related to risk in arts education, a picture emerges showing how risk is essential to learning in/through/with the arts (Babayants & Frey, 2015; Carter, Prendergast, & Belliveau, 2015; Eisner, 2002; Gallagher & Booth, 2003). This reminds us of the inherent connection between trying something new (i.e., taking a risk), where the potential for failure is not only plausible but probable (i.e., one rarely learns to read, walk, ride a bike, or succeed at a scientific experiment on the first try), and how learning is a process that is a commitment in and through time. Maxine Greene, pioneer of progressive education, suggests that rather than fearing risk, it needs to be embraced, because

> to embrace risk is to open spaces in experience for play and wonder and imagination. It involve[s] a willingness to face the unpredictable and, at once, work[s] to identify a range of untapped possibilities. [Risk allows us to] look at things as if they could be otherwise ... To take a risk is to open multiple unexplored spaces ... To take a risk is to refuse interference with personal growth or the efforts to transform new spaces in and around the world. (Greene, as cited in Ginsberg, 2012, p. vii)

In this quotation, rather than countering the very real potential effects of risk (i.e., exposure to harm or loss), Greene contends that it is the possibility of consequences that make risk ultimately necessary for personal growth and for the transformation of new spaces in and around the world. She even goes so far as to suggest that one must embrace risk in order to open up new spaces of wonder. The importance of risk-taking to learning, especially in relationship to subjects with creative outcomes, is so significant that *Theatre and Learning* (Babayants & Frey, 2015) has an entire section dedicated to discussing the relationship between taking risks and learning through theatre. These chapters have very different understandings of what taking risks mean in the theatre and drama education context. A review of the literature related to risk and learning in drama education and theatre (Babayants & Frey, 2015; McKinnon & Upton, 2015; Perry, 2015; Wager, 2015) reveals three subcategories on risk that best help to deepen understandings about the kinds of risk described in the vignettes: socio-emotional risk, student-centred teaching, and reframing failure.

Personal Socio-Emotional Risk

There are numerous examples of how participants in the vignettes took personal socio-emotional risks throughout the creation process and during performances. Socio-emotional in this instance refers to the way(s) that individuals had to have or develop self-awareness, joint-attention, understanding of the perspectives of others, a healthy level of self-esteem, and the ability to regulate their emotions. In the literature, socio-emotional development is usually within the domain of child development, in relationship to theories of attachment, and socio-emotional risk-taking is discussed in relation to the increased hormones of teenagers during adolescence (Tuhuwai Smith et al., 2013). In this context, taking socio-emotional risks entails examining one's thoughts, feelings, ideas, and self. Once this personal reflection takes place, sharing or re-examining with others in the drama/theatre space is another kind of risk. In the original transcripts, this term "socio-emotional risk" emerged but did not resoundingly stand out for its frequency of use. However, the descriptions of the participants' experiences illustrate how they were engaging in activities that required them to take new risks that were specific to their socio-emotional states, and where they were in their personal and creative journeys. This risk continuum looked different for each individual because it began with their own personal learning process.

In the first vignette, for example, Arlene had difficulty attending class because of anxiety but ultimately overcame her fears and performed a monologue because she wanted to be a better teacher. For Teresa, her baseline was how she had sugar-coated the teaching of Aboriginal issues to non-Aboriginal students and teachers during her practicum because she didn't want to offend others. She took a personal risk by sharing a part of her own experiences of school in her Mohawk community through the content she included in her monologue. After this performance, she commented that she felt more prepared to "take the opportunity in my own future teaching to share the truth when I'm asked to because of the personal risks I took in this drama course." The "socio-emotional risks" that Arlene and Teresa took while engaging in drama and theatre were like the ones discussed by Wager (2015) in her work with marginalized street engaged youth using applied theatre during a partnership with Vancouver Youth Visions Coalition and the University of British Columbia. In this example, socio-emotional risk is discussed through the term "resistance."

In Wager's (2015) research, youth participating in a devised theatre project take a risk by being a part of a theatre community. This means attending and participating in a joint theatre activity, and later performing for the public. Some of these youth continually resisted the drama activities that were a part of the rehearsal process and the building of a devised piece because this work included building a community with the other actors. This kind of community development represented a disruption to the lives of the youth who were living in shelters. In their lives up until being a part of this production, many of them had not experienced stability or being accountable for their actions on a regular basis. They resisted being a part of the rehearsal process because it was a risk to socially-emotionally open up and engage with others. As also identified in the first vignette, simply showing up, and opening up, can be a risk.

In the second vignette, Alayna talked to the participants about taking socio-emotional risks when engaging with the TRC in relation to "white fragility and social justice stuff … it was something like: If you don't move, you won't feel your chains. I think what was just mentioned about finding a way to be a part of the conversation and doing this 'in a good way' is hard. It takes risk, which means we're going to have to learn to be ok with making mistakes sometimes, but those are the limits or chains we didn't know we had before. We have to try if change is going to happen."

In this quotation, taking a risk involves both tackling a difficult topic – the systemic perpetuation of racism vis-à-vis white privilege – as well as performing for the public. Allan's comments, previously discussed, about doing the work in order to then teach about social justice topics, also remind us that when working towards a more equitable world, everyone needs to be a part of the change. This overarching message – that we all need to be a part of making positive change in the world and that this may be at the expense of our own personal socio-emotional (or even monetary and cultural) levels of comfort – is what doing this work means. What these examples suggest is that even when socio-emotional risks exist in relation to learning in/through drama and theatre, participants seem more likely to be able to rise above their own fears if there is a significant reason for doing so. The curricular implication of this understanding means that teachers have to be willing, open, and able to explore socially significant topics such as white fragility, residential schools, appropriation, systemic racism, and classism more deeply within their classrooms. When educators are prepared to do this, then students/actors are able to do so as well.

Student-Centred Teaching

In the first and third vignettes, there are specific examples of how multiple participants were motivated to take pedagogical risks in the drama education and theatre education spaces in order to shift to student-centred models of learning. This risk is different than socio-emotional risk because it is related to one's teaching identity and not one's psycho-social challenges. Student-centred teaching is a shift from a direct or banking model of teaching (Freire, 1968). This means that rather than directly depositing information in students' minds or telling them how to act or what to do, as is common in many Western theatre and teaching paradigms, instructors, directors, and teachers take a student-centred approach in their teaching and rehearsals. A student-centred approach focuses on the questions, styles of learning, and inquiries of the individual and collective in a classroom. McKinnon and Upton (2015) emphasize how learning in drama education and theatre contexts can be a liberatory practice, and not an exercise in domination. In their research, McKinnon and Upton focus on the process of putting on a production using a learner-centred approach in a university-level program where process and not product is the focus. This work is done in order to disrupt the hierarchical tendencies of the professional theatre production where the director's vision, playwright's voice, and requirements of the actor (to differ from someone with authority) are no longer normalized. When tied to assessment, McKinnon and Upton (2015) argue that the traditional theatre model is hierarchical and can be problematic. They thus argue for the use of devised theatre processes to disrupt power in theatre education programming. By focusing on the process of creation and not the assessment of the performance, where students work without a traditional director guiding them, they have found that "true collaborative creativity (can) begin ... because ... the director-less rehearsal room alleviate[s] fear and inhibition ... and leads students to feel ownership of their own learning" (p. 129). This description of the director-less rehearsal room and the use of devised theatre processes resonate with the approaches Alayna, Jennifer, and I used, where the actors were given space and permission to explore and co-create the information that they wished or needed to explore personally in relation to the identified themes, and then they incorporated these explorations as content into the final scripts and performances.

Risk in this instance is taken on by the instructor, who challenges rehearsal processes and production outcomes by giving this work over to the student/actor, and by the student, who must take their own learning in hand. This student-directed devised theatre approach complements the socio-emotional risks that participants took because of their (often) personal motivations to explore social justice issues through theatre. Jennifer, Alayna, and I all commented on the risk that it takes to create a student-centred devised theatre piece because it means that at some point the director/instructor has to admit that they are a co-learner as well. This process, where the director/instructor models a pedagogical and personal risk, provides students with an example of how to become open and vulnerable to learning.

These examples illustrate that in order to apply a student-centred learning approach, the instructor/director has to open themselves up to the unknown. The challenge with this, through devised theatre processes in this instance, is that there is a seemingly higher probability for failure for instructor and student because devised theatre requires students to share and co-create the content for the final production. Specifically, asking students to be the centre of their own learning is asking them to take more responsibility for its outcomes because their own questions and inquiries are guiding the action in the learning space. The teacher is taking a risk by not relying on a standardized curriculum or script that dictates outcomes that can be measured quantitatively. Instructors must continually reframe expectations during the learning/creating process and consider a new relationship to taking risk and what it means to trust one's co-creators.

Risk as Rupture: Reframing Failure

In *Learning with Failure*, Mia Perry (2015) discusses how we need to rethink our relationship to failure in the arts and how glitch art, which is made from technological glitches, is based on a shifting system of values that changes with different contexts and is caught up in the ideals of success and larger ideological systems. For Perry, the slippery slope between success and failure in the education context, where discourses of failure and success dominate (p. 142), is in need of reframing. She argues that rather than viewing failure as negative (i.e., below an accepted percentage of knowledge on a particular topic retained), we need to see it in a new way. She goes on to discuss how failure in art is much more complex than in standardized learning contexts, where there can be one right answer. For example, "failed" art at one period of time has been seen as a success by later generations, indicating that the measure of success at one time may not be indicative of the long-term failure of an event but rather representative of the present-day values of a society that has a changing view of what is deemed as a success or failure. Thus, rather than focusing on "success and failure" in absolutes, Perry suggests schools could be "laboratories of failure defiance" where we need to disrupt expectations and outcomes of student success and failure. When considering the function of failure in the performing arts, an even stronger rationale for learning with failure can be made. In the performing arts, failure is a part of the learning process. When one learns lines and blocking, or starts interacting with other people in an embodied way, no one can predict exactly what will happen until one is in the process of "doing." Even once blocking has been determined and opening night takes place, there are always subtle (and sometimes not-so-subtle) differences in each and every production of a show. These differences could be a result of an actor having a cold, or someone feeling upset about something before the performance on a particular night. There is no way to completely ensure that a performance will be exactly the same, and this is also the beauty of drama and theatre. It is an embodied human art form, where there is no "hiding" one's "mistakes" or "self" in the moment of performing "someone/thing else."

Both "failures" and "successes" in the drama education and theatre contexts can lead to a connection with an inner vulnerability that is beyond one's conscious perception of self because there is an exposure of one's conscious and subconscious selves that moves beyond the mind-body divide (Carter, 2014a). Through collective creation processes, we not only risk failure or making mistakes but also being cared for, seen, and loved. We risk being fully human, and with this, the lines of failure and success are no longer causal and dualistic in nature, but simultaneous and essential for processes of becoming and being. In this way, theatre does more than "open us to the potential for failure"; rather, as Perry (2015) discusses, it has the potential to rupture our relationship(s) with ourselves, our worlds, and others. Deleuze and Guattari (1987) call a "rupture," or how an alternative can emerge in the process of schooling/learning, an opportunity to lead one to multiple modes of representation or learning outcomes. Rethinking risk as rupture in the projected path of learning is an important way of understanding the third theme of "risk" because, by and large, the performances highlighted in this book exemplify the experiences of participants who viewed "failure" as "ruptures" within the creation process. It is this reframing of "failure" to "creative rupture" that, I suggest, ultimately allows the participants to engage in the creation process.

For example, if Alayna had measured the success of *Sing the Brave Song: This Isn't Over!* by meeting the initial expectations she had for the play rehearsal and process, she would have viewed the final production as a failure because she did not find the actors that she was seeking during the first call and this delayed her original rehearsal schedule. When she did cast the show, she had a cast of white actors who were not comfortable with playing the roles of the diverse characters that she had created. Rather than continuing along as planned, she reworked the play through a devised process with the participants. This shows how rather than seeing the hurdles along the way as "failures" of her original vision, she was able to view them as "ruptures." These ruptures disrupted her original plan(s) and led to alternative end points. Our conversations about creativity helped us understand how Alayna turned what could have been viewed as failures into ruptures or opportunities.

In the example of *Sing the Brave Song*, creativity as an antidote to the fear of change meant that rather than giving up or admitting "failure" when the play casting and rehearsal process didn't go as anticipated, Alayna adapted and created an alternative. Her past experiences working on genocide theatre productions are a part of the reason that she had a resilient disposition when working on *Sing the Brave Song*. This is evidenced by her comment, "But ... and it's a big but ... at one point, people are going to criticize. Like I said, this is not my first rodeo, so I'm like: Cool. I anticipate some things [are going] to happen ... there are going to be critiques, but this is just an opportunity for a conversation." This example of building her own capacity for creative resilience can also be considered building creative-embodied capital through a rupture/ failure. But how does creativity link with rupture, learning, and risk?

Creativity

Despite the plethora of definitions for creativity in education, economics, business, arts, and aesthetics literature, the search for a universally agreed-upon one is, as Salehi (2008) concludes, non-existent. Yet Salehi agrees with Cropley (1999) that creativity is more than "a matter of cognitive processes such as knowing, thinking, recognizing, remembering, or puzzling out ... it involves factors such as motivation, personal properties, and feelings" (p. 517).

A part of the challenge of defining creativity is that while it was once relegated to the domain of artists and the unknown aspects of human aesthetic engagements and creations, it has most recently been taken up as a method for moving towards increased innovation for purposes of production, tied to discourses around creative economies (Araya & Peters, 2010) and industries. Harris (2014) connects this recent shift in discourse around creativity in education to a gentrification of the imaginary where the arts are being colonized by neo-liberal ideologies and the needs of the global marketplace. Thus, rather than simply being concerned about what it means to take creative risks in arts education, there is a concern that true creative exploration is as anathema to the global neo-liberal culture (Halberstam, 2011). In relation to arts education contexts, creativity is not only "the production of novel and useful ideas by an individual or a small group of individuals working together" (Amabile & Pratt, 2016, as cited in Fischer & Golden, 2018, p. 13), it can be a critical undertaking that has economic and political ramifications. This conversation can be applied to students or teachers working together on a creative endeavour and differs from early creativity studies that distinguished between only two types of creativity: eminent/ big "C" Creativity, which is domain-changing, and everyday/little "c" creativity. In the context of education, scholars now recognize that there is a creative continuum that goes from the everyday workings of the classroom through to teacher initiatives that effect entire departments, schools, and communities (Bramwell et al., 2011; Craft, 2002; Reilly et al., 2011; Worth, 2000, 2010).

However, rather than focusing on the vast and emerging literature on creativity, I'd like to emphasize this term based on its significance to learning through the arts and the way(s) that it promotes taking risks as a part of its process-based, emergent, and iterative nature. In this context, critical/creative work "happens in the hard work of execution (and not through bursts of inspiration)" (Sawyer, 2006, p. 21). This idea of working on a creative project over time connects to a notion of "creativity as becoming." According to Harris (2014), the importance of fostering spaces where failures are viewed as acceptable – indeed welcomed – by those who understand their generative power not just as part of the "process" of learning and inventing/expressing but as ends in themselves, is increasingly critical, since there are so few outside the creative arts classroom. Harris (2014) argues this point even further:

> It is because of the slow global spread of standardisation ... that these spaces and places for experimentation are drying up and that the rhetoric of creativity is increasing in relation to schools and education. Yet the conflation of creativity with innovation is a form of ideological gentrification, in that while appearing to value the arts and creative endeavour it is really redirecting and narrowing the discourse of creativity into productive innovation and marketplace measures of value. And this more than anything signals the death knell of "arts education," which remains tainted by its relationship to risk, un-productivity (time-wasting, daydreaming) and "failure" – all of which are increasingly impossible in a marketplace economy. (pp. 18–20)

Never before has the "right to fail" or to be creative been so complicated, and simultaneously so important, perhaps becoming the most valuable commodity in the twenty-first-century marketplace (Harris, 2014, p. 3).

This new economic (and political) relationship in which creativity is being commodified for the needs of global profit margins makes it significant in discourses around risk in arts educational contexts because of the ethical responsibilities teachers have for now fostering critical creativity in educational contexts. A part of the way of supporting teachers in this work is to help them to build communities of support within the educational contexts that they are working within and to potentially connect creativity outcomes to transdisciplinary objectives.

Theme 2: Belonging

Community

Throughout the vignettes, the theme of community emerged as central to the creation of a performance. For Jennifer, "the most important thing (for putting on a production) is to have community support" in order to ensure that a theatre in education production is a success. In an educational/classroom context, John Dewey's ideas on the great community, remind us that the possibilities and potentials of fostering a great community can be transformative, but that there are conditions that need to exist:

> For a community to exist as something other than an association or organization that is based on people getting together around common needs or goals, a trust needs to be developed. This trust based on natural association occurs as a result of mutual respect and is suggested to occur organically. Dewey's second condition for a great community is mutual benefit. This means that everyone in a community is growing as a result of being in it (with an ideal benefit being an individual's experience of freedom as a result of the trust they feel). This is a result of not only the possession and distribution of social knowledge (the third condition) but of this knowledge leading to active participation of all members being able to help direct the community with which they are a part (fourth condition). As one might guess, this would lead to the full integration of individuals in a community (fifth condition) and then subsequently, their ability to communicate through a series of signs and shared symbols (sixth condition). (Carter, 2014, p. 240)

This description of the great community is one which I have viewed as an ideal to aspire to in my own classroom teaching because it values shared communication, trust, the development of knowledge, and mutual benefit. In my teaching, in order to foster such a community, I have sought to use activities with students that help them to develop truth with themselves, with one another, and with me so that the co-constructed

learning space we share is one in which they feel they can actively participate in in a variety of ways (Mreiwed et al., 2017; Shabtay et al., 2019).
Thus, I have viewed developing a classroom community as the essential
solution for fostering creative risk-taking in the drama education classroom, linking the themes of risk and community naturally together during the cross-comparative analysis of information within the vignettes.
Perhaps because of my bias towards the importance of fostering classroom community, I recognized its characteristics and significance within
the research early on when observing and interviewing participants.

To understand the significance of the theme of community in educational settings, I also turned to the literature on communities of practice
(CoPs) in the previous chapter. By working together on authentic tasks,
CoPs evolved to include like-minded participants who can collaborate
over time. In the vignettes, the idea of a CoP provided the actors, direc-
tor/playwright, teachers, producer, and stage manager with an authentic
opportunity to work together in a supported environment (i.e., the time
and space of the rehearsal/theatre production and performance) to
explore new pedagogical paradigms (i.e., the challenges of implementing the TRC). It is not a stretch to say that I am completely and utterly
convinced that drama education can help to build classroom community
and that the research in this book supports the theme of community as
something that is essential for putting on a successful theatre in education event so that pedagogical and personal risks can take place. So, why is
the theme of belonging, and not community, the heading of this section?

To consider this question, I turn to the personal to describe my own
initial rationalization for focusing on building community that began
when I started to question my analysis of the purported benefits. A part
of the concern that arose in relation to this questioning is the time it
takes to build and maintain relationships – and not just relationships
that are in place for a short period of time, like those within a six-week
course or two-year granting cycle. I wondered: "If the larger focus of this
book is on teacher agency and what it means to explore social justice
work, do the ways in which community is spoken about need to be reconsidered in order to really honour the ideas and people who have given
their time, thoughts, bodies, and emotions to this work?"

This question prompted a memory of being asked to draw the concept
of "time" at a dinner party twenty years ago. After each person had completed their picture, we showed our images to one another. There were
several clocks and watches, and a few timelines with key moments from
one's life experiences. I had drawn a circle with the changing seasons and
sun and moon, which was different because of the cyclical nature of my
representation and its connection to different phases from the natural

world. This artful inquiry returned to me as I thought about the theme of community, and how community and learning seem to have recently become wrapped up for me in a linear progression. For Dewey, education is "the reconstruction or reorganization of experience which adds to the meaning of experience, and which increases the ability to direct the course of subsequent experience" (1998, p. 76). This definition of education may be problematic (like my long-held view of community) because learners are asked to reconfigure an experience or relationship in order to create an educational future that might be more directable. Some might suggest that such reorganization depends on a fuller understanding of who we are in time and place, in relation to other languages, cultures, and people. This is in part about control and the creation of a particular kind of community for a particular end. But what if the initial premise of time and the way relationships are constructed is flawed? What if education is not about moving from experience to experience along a seemingly linear continuum, within like-minded communities? What if the goal is not a goal at all and focusing on something as arbitrary as teacher agency is as inconsequential as the individual human being themselves?

This philosophical conundrum around community gave me pause to consider what led me to this research and the threads that had begun to connect between me and other people, places, ideas, and theories. I began to realize that at the core of community was belonging, or feeling connected through time, and that this was also at the heart of my own personal inquiries, that "one of the great values of belonging to any group with a purpose is that we act with other people, for the benefit of other people, knowing that we could not accomplish anything without other people" (Clarkson, 2014, p. 73).

From the ages of six to fifteen, I lived in Thunder Bay, Ontario, Canada, and gazed every day at the shape of Nanabush, Nanabojo, or The Sleeping Giant – a peninsula in Lake Superior that looks like a giant lying on its back. Gazing on Nanabush from my bedroom window, from the school yard, or while riding the bus to school gave me great comfort because I used to think that if anything happened to me near Thunder Bay or on Lake Superior, the giant would wake up and help. Perhaps this thought was in part because of the Ojibwe stories that describe Nanabush as a shape-shifting "trickster" who, as legend goes, turned to stone when the location of a silver mine was disclosed to white settlers. Perhaps it was because I liked to walk on the snow-covered ice of Lake Superior in the winter, only partially knowing if it was safe to do so, and I found solace in the idea that he would wake if I was in danger and save me. Regardless of the exact reason for my feelings, this land mass, and swimming in the waters of Lake Superior, made me feel safe and at home, that I belonged in nature and that I was a part of it. When throwing rocks into Lake Superior last summer with my own sons, I retold the story of "The Sleeping Giant" to them.

It was after sharing this story that I was reminded of Richard Wagamese's *One Drum* and "the smallest circles first" teaching introduced in Chapter 1 (Lorraine, as cited in Wagamese, 2019 p. 80). Perhaps because we are both from northwestern Ontario, I feel a strong connection to Wagamese's works. Perhaps it is a result of something deeper that is a mystery within us all, and his work invites me to pay attention to the feelings and relationships that speak about connection and belonging with/in the private, public, personal, spiritual, physical, and metaphysical spaces, where with respect to what is eternal, there is no difference between being possible and being (Aristotle, ca. 350 B.C.E./2013).

Being, Affect, Anishenabeg, and Belonging

Thus, when I question if the ripples of the small circle I have created through my life and work are making enough of a difference, fast enough, within my own "margins of manoeuvrability" (Massumi, 2015, p. 3), I return to the "start with the smallest circles first" teaching and the "circles within circles" metaphor that was used to conceptualize the data in Vignette 3. This shift to the circular rather than the linear disrupts the construction of community for me and replaces it with belonging. Belonging is more than having an association or membership within a community. Belonging is wrapped up in Being and not relegated to the learning experiences we offer in classrooms that are premised upon a progression towards mastery of skills. Belonging means being open to affect, or the power to affect or be affected. For Massumi (2015), "affect" is defined as hope, when thinking about where one is able to go and what one might be able to do. To "hope" is the power to affect and to be affected when belonging in an interconnected way that is not measured by mutual commitment to a task or ideology or goal (or a specific community that can also exclude). In Spanish, hope, or *esperar*, is a verb meaning hope that is always an action rather than the more passive definition for hope in English, which is an expectation or desire for/of something. To belong. To affect. To love. To hope. These actions of being are not requirements for participation in certain communities, where some people can be excluded or included based on values or actions. They are about core connections, they are Being-singular-plural, *Anishenabeg*, agape.

If as Nancy (2000) suggests, Being is meaning in and of itself, and our lives (Being) can only be understood in relation to a singular-plural coexistence, then all affects we experience singularly are interconnected acts of hope that affect ourselves and others in, through, and beyond time. This means that there can be no difference between being possible and being when considering the eternal (and everything is eternal). Wagamese's (2019) definition of *Anishenabeg* as *all the people, all our relations* (p. 43) is like interdependence among everything, in this life and the next. If someone in my community is hurting, I will hurt. We need to work together across communities so that "one form of life exists in relationship with all other forms, so that a bear or a salmon can become a human being or a tree. This is the most concrete and powerful iteration of the interdependence that we call belonging to each other, being part of a whole. The circle opens to include us, for better or worse. The circle implies a common fate that we share and that we acknowledge. Your destiny is my destiny" (Clarkson, 2014, p. 8). And so, belonging is being with an ongoing commitment to hope.

This means that interpretations about the personal and public need to be reconsidered if one lives the inner and outer as a hopeful affect. Massumi (2015) considers this contention as follows:

> To affect and to be affected is to be open to the world, to be active in it and to be patient for its return activity … One always affects and is affected by encounters; which is to say, through events. To begin affectively in change is to begin in relation, and to begin in relation is to begin in the event … The concept of affect is "transversal," in Deleuze and Guattari's understanding of that term. This means that it cuts across the usual categories. Prime among these are the categories of the subjective and objective. Although affect is all about intensities of feeling, the feeling process cannot be characterized as exclusively subjective or objective; the encounters through which it passes strike the body as immediately as they stir the mind … Thinking the transversally of affect requires that we fundamentally rethink all of these categories (and concepts) in ways that include them in the event together. (p. ix)

I return to Wagamese (2019) to think about how affect implicates Being-singular-plural in another way, through Anishenabeg. As mentioned earlier, I grew up in northwestern Ontario, and my immediate and extended family still live in Thunder Bay, Wabigoon, Vermillion Bay, Red Lake, Keewatin, and Ignace. Many of my earliest experiences were shaped by teachings from the Ojibwe, Cree, and Oji-Cree people who lived in and around the places I grew up, and by my family, some of whom are Cree and Metis. In school in Kenora, Thunder Bay, and Dryden, I remember always feeling included when sitting in circles as sage was burned at the start of a ceremony before stories were told about the importance of tobacco; when being taught how to make birch bark art; or when being invited to make bannock. I was welcomed to participate in pow-wows in the summer and to wonder and wander in the bush. I felt included and accepted as "myself" during these activities. When on solo camping trips or when spending time on the land, the moose, deer, wolves, birds, and bears were sometimes the only creatures I communicated with for days. The feelings of acceptance or belonging during these times were in contrast to the feelings I felt at church and school if I didn't have pretty enough clothes, or if I just wanted to run outside in my bare feet after a service in the rain, rather than sitting and eating cake or drinking tea in a silly dress. I always thought, in my basic understanding of Ojibwe, that *Anishenabeg* meant all Indigenous people. This made me feel that I didn't belong in the places/spaces that made me feel "at home." Wagamese's description of this term changed this reading of space and place for me, when he described how *Anishenabeg* means all living beings, and for the first time I felt like I belonged.

If hope/affect is, as Massumi (2015) suggests, all about intensities of feeling, and if the feeling process cannot be characterized as exclusively subjective or objective, the transversality of affect requires that we fundamentally rethink all categories where public/private are all complicated together within a shared affect of Being-singular-plural. This means that being "present in the willingness to act and speak at all, to insert oneself into the world and begin a story of one's own" (Arendt, as cited in Clarkson, 2014, p. 60) no longer means leaving one's private world and entering the public one because they are one and the same. Belonging is the deep essential hope that one experiences in connection to all things. Anishenabeg. Affecting and being affected by experiences is not a choice, it is a part of belonging and offering one's own truth when speaking or action is in season. It is feeling a part of a pulse that is in and beyond our singular-plural Being.

During a performance, belonging is felt in the silence and stillness between breaths as the actor exhales and we all know how simple and fragile life is. The ritualistic roots of the theatre speak to the reasons people came together for collective catharsis through laughter, tears, and moments of transcendence by witnessing on stage the impossible becoming possible. In this way, drama education and theatre is an opportunity to co-construct personal/public affects/acts of hope as a curriculum of becoming through belonging.

Theme 3: Counter-Narratives

The pedagogical challenge is that counter-stories have been forgotten or suppressed: "Teaching ... has to deal not so much with lack of knowledge as with resistances to knowledge" (Felman, 1982, p. 30). In order for white teachers to overcome resistance, they need opportunities to

(a) revisit their literacy memoirs, in social contexts with other teachers, to perceive that the "cauldron of stories" is bound by implicit criteria of inclusion and exclusion; (b) re-experience and acknowledge the significance to them, personally and professionally; and (c) experience "counter-stories" that challenge the "master story" implicit in the "cauldron" of stories (Strong-Wilson, 2007, p. 124).

The focus of this theme is on the importance of including counter or unsettling narratives in the experiences of teaching and learning in the Quebec curriculum so that a disruption of certain unquestioned knowledges can take place. As illustrated in this research, when these ruptures occur, pedagogical agency can result, which makes the case for an ongoing curriculum of becoming(s) that produce affect. This means that, as discussed in the first two themes, the ability to affect and to be affected is tied up in what it means to belong, and the provocations or ruptures that produce affects, such as the unsettling narratives like learning about residential schools for the first time, are prioritized by learners and educators. When this takes place, learning is not about understanding how to shift an individual's perceptions, emotions, or creative engagements with critical societal problems in thoughtful and proactive ways, it is about centring new understandings of Being and becoming(s) through hope.

However, in action what sometimes seems to happen in my experience is that there is fear around this work. When talking about preparing to produce *Sing the Brave Song: This Isn't Over!* and conducting rehearsals, actors discussed feelings of uncertainty and fear about learning about the counter-narratives to settler history. They, as an all-white cast, were afraid of doing or saying the wrong thing. In relation to white fragility, this fear of saying the wrong thing can lead to the avoidance of important conversations and deeper learning about topics of significance. Trust needs to be established, and a sense of belonging to a conversation that needs to happen needs to take place, so that deeper engagements with important topics can win out over fear. This is a process and a commitment. Here are parts of that conversation:

JULIANNA: I personally felt more and more comfortable as I learned more and more and had a better understanding of the actual issues themselves ... during my audition, Alayna said, "What do you know about this?" and I said, "Not enough." That was kind of where I started with this. So, I felt more comfortable taking on this material as I learned more about it.

JULIE: Before the play, I had a global understanding of the topics we explored, and then there were just a ton of gaps in my understanding. And the understandings I had were very general ... but, again, I only learned ... I wouldn't even say "learned" ... I only found out about residential schooling in CEGEP [General and Vocational College], which is what? Three years ago.

As Julianna and Julie discuss during a focus group, they had general understandings of what some of the topics to be explored in *Sing the Brave Song* were, although they didn't name anything specific, beyond residential schools. Jesse came to this work thinking about the topics explored in the play as events that had happened, and not about the implications that particular events had on realities in current Canada, such as the higher than average number of Indigenous people incarcerated or living in poverty.

This opportunity to actually have an unsettling conversation in the theatre rehearsal context changed the way Jesse began to engage with what is going on in his "real" life. In this way, a goal of using drama education and theatre to explore critical societal issues provides participants with an opportunity to affect and be affected by an intensity that connects them to others and themselves in a new way. The importance of creating a space for this critical and creative work is described as necessary by Julianna through her critique of the way Indigenous content was learned in her Canadian history class:

[My history course] dealt with a lot of issues, but it was just snippets and, we never asked: "Why are things important? Why is listening to this person speak important? And why is their representation here important?" It was nothing that really delved into the meat of it, and so I think that the content in the play really gave a holistic understanding of things. This opportunity to delve "into the meat" of a topic by socio-emotionally engaging with it and framing it through the lens of reconciliation helped me frame my previously limited understandings about Indigenous-settler relations, because I feel like this gives me, as a white person, a place in the conversation ... because otherwise these issues are so big and we just ask, "How do we solve them?" And that feels so overwhelming and big to take on and too big to think about.

Unsettling Pedagogies and Responsibilities

As discussed in the methodology section of this book, this research was framed through arts-based educational research that relied on narrative and curriculum theories. Beyond thinking about narrative within the research context to enact teacher agency, Bruner (2002) encourages theorists and practitioners alike to understand all aspects of life narratively because what is socially good depends on a strong valuation of the human being, who is free to grow and develop individually and as a part of a collective. Such a process is vital to agency because in the sharing of stories, whether remembered or created, professional identities can be enhanced, and we have the opportunity to know and understand the particularities of our communities with greater clarity amid difference.

As the three vignettes in this book illustrate, this suggestion is easily written but more challenging to follow. It takes an ongoing commitment to communicate with others who come from different backgrounds, cultures, and communities to learn truth(s) and tackle our responsibilities in relationship to reconciliation. It is an ongoing challenge to learn that the work of reconciliation never ends and that aligning practices with values may take a complete shift of one's body, mind, and spirit. However, as learners physically, intellectually, emotionally, and metaphysically explore the curriculum together through the arts, they engage in dialogue as they create, rewrite, and breakdown/critically analyse existing and/ or new narratives. Through this process of exploration and the building of scenes and characters in the drama education and theatre contexts, issues that are relevant to students within the context of the world that they are living in become more than mere happenings that exist beyond their reach. Everything is made relevant because their experiences and those of others become a part of their own narrative as they actively address and explore them together.

Chapter Five

Full Circle

Unfoldings

This research began as a way to consider if drama education and theatre could be catalysts for enabling pre- and in-service teachers' agency around bringing Canada's Truth and Reconciliation Commission's (TRC) Calls to Action (#62 i and #63 i, ii, iii, and iv) for Education into their classrooms because "teachers are recipients insofar as they inherit the discourse put forth in teacher education programs and across the curriculum ... [but] they become interpreters of the curriculum who are in a position to reproduce, disrupt or negotiate the limitations of a singular Canadian narrative and the Settler agenda" (Brant-Birioukov et al., 2020, p. 48). While the Quebec arts curriculum and TRC offer justifiable means for the inclusion of reconciliation pedagogy in elementary to university classrooms, the experiences of the participants in the vignettes illustrate the real challenges, ethical engagements, and realities of this work. Potawatomi scholar Susan Dion describes how primarily racialized white, middle class, female teachers are in teacher education programs and the profession, and how this positionality allows for a "perfect stranger syndrome" in which Canadian educators are comfortable acknowledging Indigenous injustice, as long as they can position themselves as not a part of the system that marginalizes Indigeneity or requires personal responsibility (Dion, as cited in Brant-Birioukov et al., 2020, p. 45). Thus, active resistance to engaging in the praxis of reconciliation is a hurdle that must be overcome. In this research, the drama classroom and theatre rehearsal space provided the educational site/liminal space to "do the work" of reconciliation praxis. Decentralizing dominant settler discourses was a focus of this preliminary work as participants were exposed to counter-narratives to Canadian settler history and geography; the implications of systemic racism and colonization; feminist and post-racial theories; political, social, and economic ramifications of governmental policies; and students' own positionality and decolonizing process(es) in the development of socio-emotional connections through drama education and theatre concepts. People were changed. Relationships flourished. Cross-curricular connections were established through songs, dances, conversations, silences, deepened breaths, movements, rituals, meditations, moments, and collective catharsis.

Additional skills such as negotiation, seeing another's point of view, spatial awareness, pacing, embodied learning, self-regulation, resiliency, and empathy were also described as kinds of learning and (un)learning that took place. In this way, there was a turn in the pedagogical space distinguished by Gadamer (1997) as the difference between experience as reconstruction and experience as construction.

> Experience as reconstruction is to experience once more something that we already have experienced, and which consequently is already a part of our previous knowing. Typically, these experiences confirm our expectations, whether it is to give the correct answer to the teacher's question or to remember the teacher's instruction. Experience as construction is to make new experiences; experiences that are not yet confirmed as part of our life-world, and will consequently stand as a protest, objection or contrast to our previous experiences. (Gadamer, 1997, as cited in Schonmann, 2011, p. 24)

Experience as construction, rather than reconstruction, is one way of understanding the nature of how engaging in conversations around reconciliation in the classroom first and foremost require subjective reconstruction. This is then reinforced through active engagements and opportunities where intersubjective engagements through dialogue and art making require the individual to put their interior experience "at stake" (Gadamer, 1997/2003). This calls into question the very aims of education:

> We are accustomed to asking "What has the student learned?" The question is operationalized to mean, "What does the student know or is able to do as of, say May 12?" This conception of learning does not take into account the fact that what a student has been exposed to may interact in significant ways with what he or she will be exposed to in the future. Future experiences may confer a significance upon earlier learning that it did not initially have. (Eisner, 2002, p. 71)

If in- and pre-service teachers do not have the opportunity to engage with themselves, content, and others to make sense of how they are responsible for reconciliation, their future experiences in the classroom and beyond will be forever affected. If learning is seen as a representation of what one is able to regurgitate on a particular day and time, the ethical and embodied significance of relationality and time needed for personal processing can potentially cause harm and prematurely put an end to the process of teacher reconceptualization as they seek to represent unfolding understandings.

Towards an Instructional Model for Belonging and Becoming by Learning through/with Drama

Table 5.1 summarizes how learning individually and collectively through drama education and theatre occurred in the vignettes. The purpose of tracking and synthesizing the instruction, tools, and intended learning that took place within the vignettes is to illustrate how the findings in this research can be extended and used by practitioners with their own students. Along these lines, the full scripts for *Sing the Brave Song: This Isn't Over!* and *Reconciliation!* are included in appendixes 1 and 2, respectively. Full permission for the use of each script has been provided by the creators of each play, so that anyone wishing to engage further with this work can do so using these resources as a starting point.

As illustrated in Table 5.1, the guided learning that primarily functioned within the parameters of the arts curriculum first focused on the individual. Learning was then reinforced in the public realm through active engagement with specific drama activities and tools with the cast/drama class. The overarching principles of openness to ruptures, working together to make the theatre space one of belonging, working towards a collective performance, and collaborating and understanding the intent of engaging in reconciliatory praxis emphasize the significance of the learning conditions that this work takes place within.

Drama and theatre are particularly well-suited pedagogical spaces for exploring and introducing teachers and students to their responsibilities for taking up the calls in the TRC because, as Fiske (1999) presents in *Champions of Change: The Impact of the Arts on Learning*, the arts can:

- reach students who are not otherwise being reached
- reach students in ways that they are not otherwise being reached
- connect students to themselves and each other and at the same time provide new challenges for those students already considered successful
- transform the environment for learning

Table 5.1. Towards an Instructional model for belonging and becoming by learning through/with drama

Potential learners	Cross-cutting purpose of learning	Guided learning processes tools		Designing instruction	Intended learning
		Centre self	and Collective engagement	The environment	Learning aims to develop learner's:
Pre-service teachers	To foster teacher agency through arts curriculum to learn and teach the TRC Calls to Action	• Start with the KAIROS Blanket Exercise, facilitated by a community Elder • Dialogue led by community Elder	• Forum Theatre • Reader's Theatre • Creation of scenes and monologues • Newspaper theatre • Object elicitation	• Includes instructional activities that provide an opportunity for personal and collective risk-taking/ruptures • Considers student perspectives as a starting place for learning • Teaching is interactive	• Understanding of the past, in relation to Calls to Action in the TRC, and to have a sensitivity towards it in relation to the lived experiences of those with a different positionality
In-service teachers		Learning about IRSs in McGill class led to teacher agency. Promise to herself and future students to continue to learn and share information about IRSs.	• Devised theatre • KAIROS Blanket Exercise and ongoing dialogue(s) with Elder • University/school/community partnership model.	• Books, music, dance to build scenes • Indigenous musicians, community members, dancers taught students	
Settler or newcomer actors		Started by asking: What do you know about the TRC? Individuals brought in summary of TRC, headlines, etc.	• Writing process that accounts for actor positionality • Debates, conversations, etc. reflected in performance • Characters represented actors' questions about the TRC	• Newspaper theatre • Play-building activities • Focus on ethical realities • Purpose of production: inform about TRC	

Additional Learning and Guiding Principles
- openness to ruptures
- theatre space as a place of belonging
- collective goal of presenting to others
- need for ongoing collaboration with community members and Indigenous knowledge keepers
- importance of intent

- provide learning opportunities for the adults in the lives of young people
- connect learning experiences to the world of real work. (Fiske, 1999 p. ix)

More recently, Bamford's (2009) international research found that arts-rich education contributes to both social and emotional well-being as well as academic achievement in the arts and more broadly. As many scholars have argued (Prentki & Stinson, 2016; Saunders, 2021), the arts are not an optional addition to the core curriculum: they are core curriculum, and a human right, as outlined by the United Nations. This argument is based on studies, such as the longitudinal work of Catterall (2002), who documents the long-term, positive impacts of the arts on students from low and high socio-economic backgrounds.

Learning Responsibilities

This research also points to a need to end the reification in drama education of "walking a mile in someone else's shoes" because of the harm that appropriative actions can have when this statement is taken up uncritically. For example, if an actor uses blackface (i.e., non-Black people darkening their faces to portray Black people) in theatre contexts, research has found that there is an intensified social pleasure for blackface wearers and for their audiences because of the ways that this choice pushes the limits of acceptable racial discourse (Howard, 2018). This example speaks to a larger issue around attunement and appreciation in acting contexts, where disabled actors are also asking able-bodied performers not to portray them and their unique disabilities on stage or screen. This means the following questions need to be asked:

- What does respecting historically marginalized people's experiences mean for drama and theatre education?
- How does intention affect the actor's subjective bracketing process when creating a character in order to "step into someone else's shoes"?
- Is it ethical for a human to perform as non-human animal, in order to understand posthuman phenomenology through performance?

If, as participants in Vignettes 2 and 3 contend, learning about the TRC Calls to Action for Education through drama must begin with the individual, then subjectivity and intersubjectivity cannot be intertwined, though deep engagement with both are essential in reconciliation pedagogical work. This means that using the phenomenological reduction to under-stand and theorize the experiences of the individual creating a character in a drama education context has limits because the traditional phenom-enological process conflates the subjective and intersubjective (Carter, 2016). In Carter (2016), Autophenomenology (A) is proposed as a means to allow one to question one's own questions through grounded phenom-enological questioning (Magrini, 2014) by separating the first step of the phenomenological reduction from "subjective" to "subjective" auto- (a) and "intersubjective" hetero- (h). This emphasis allows for the exploration of teacher identity, internal and external, as a path towards changing the educational institution and becoming an epistemic subject. This step is important because phenomenology's focus on seeing something for the first time, without accounting for subjectivity or embodied experiences on the level of consciousness, does not require one to address hegemony and colonization in the internal and external territories of identity. In order to truly "see something as if for the first time" the individual must under-stand an experience from a new perspective that takes into account their own deeply rooted prejudices or positions, and this cannot take place by "stepping into someone else's shoes" if that person/thing/object/human does not want their story to be told. In this way, the Autophenomeno-logical bracketing process is a posthuman phenomenology because the human is not (necessarily) the centre of being or becoming. Rather, an understanding of the other's alterity may require looking to the narratives and teachings of objects, stories, places, animals, and so on through a lens of agential realism. This requires respect, study, and turning over ideas, stories, narratives, feelings, bodies, and so forth again and again and again through conversations and performances within communities of practice that may become sites of belonging, shared relational meaning, and ac-countability. This also means that sometimes there are stories, objects, and traditions that cannot be told or retold. In this way, Autophenomenology diverges from the posthuman phenomenology of Lewis and Owen (2020) who use posthuman phenomenology to perform the non-human animal in order to experience a deeper ecology of landscape. This is done with-out asking or considering the animal they seek to embody if this is ethically responsible. Autophenomenology sits with a view of posthuman phenom-enology that seeks to open spaces rather than to occupy them.

In teacher education, these sites of belonging are needed because often-times pre- and in-service teachers only question and reflect on information and events that reinforce their previously held world views. As Jan Hare contends, this protects the innocence and privilege of the settler, and rec-onciliation becomes a conceptual understanding that leads to absolution, rather than redress (2020). In this respect, settlers play an important role in

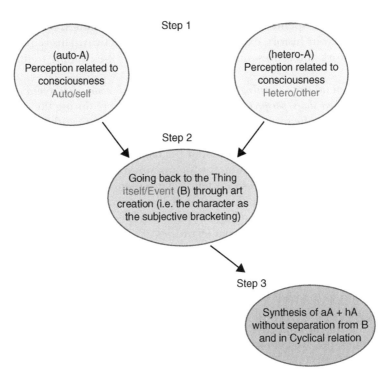

Image 5.1. Autophenomenological (A) proposal for understanding how monologues and performance can create learning encounters of affect (hope) that foreground positionality of participants (where spaces are opened rather than occupied). Source: Created by the author.

reconciliation: teacher education programs and curriculum must include participation, so that reconciliation becomes more than a trend (Hare, 2020, p. 22). Spending time intentionally with one's positionality was seen in the experiences of the individual participants in the vignettes, who were open to learning more deeply about their responsibilities for reconciliation by unpacking privilege and bias. Once individual learning took place, participants were prepared to engage in discussing or learning topics with others and making connections between experiences/territories.

Step 1 (aA + hA) of Autophenomenology maps onto the participant experiences described in the vignettes. Specific learning techniques used by participants and their relevance to Step 1 are illustrated in Table 5.1. The following is a summation of the Autophenomenological (A) process as it applies to the model for teaching and learning reconciliation praxis using drama and theatre:

Step 1: (Part 1) Spend time *walking in your own shoes* (**auto-A,** self) to understand your history, experience, identity, subjectivity. This is individual work and represented in Table 5.1 under the heading Centre self.

(Part 2) Spend time *learning from someone/thing else about what it means to walk in their shoes/perspectives/stories* (**hetero-A,** other) during the devising and/or rehearsal process. This requires interaction and is represented in Table 5.1 under the heading Collective Engagement.

Step 2: After or overlapping with Step 1, a character and devised piece are co-created. Consideration for the intention of the artistic engagement, shared experiences with fellow participants/actors, and mindful and ongoing consultation with collaborators must occur. Step 2 requires dwelling within a liminal space of hope and becoming, beyond the internal and external territories of identity. This is the space of creation.

Step 3: There is an opportunity during Step 3 to understand the effect of Steps 1 and 2 on being, becoming, and belonging. This step brings together diverse voices, perspectives, and experiences together into a hopeful and shared space. In the vignettes, this step represents the collective performances and audience engagements in which the work no longer belongs to the cast or a single actor: it is a shared gift.

This Autophenomenological framework is proposed as a way to account for the significant understandings that were articulated by participants and collaborators during this research. This is not linear work: it is relational, and presenting it through a step-by-step process may take away from the recursive nature of this potentially iterative process because of the emergent understandings that may occur in Step 3 when an audience views and responds to the performance. This requires a commitment from participants to continually live relational engagements as becoming(s) and affects (i.e., performances of engagements with hope), which are essential for teachers who are victims of their training in that they are often taught to instruct, but not to engage. There is tension in representing a "synthesis" of the research and stories shared in this book through the format of a table and in these steps. It is unsettling to frame knowledge in these forms which seem to attempt to simplify, for the purposes of reproduction, the rich experiences, dialogues, and artistic creations that were embodied affects for the participants and myself. And so, the "conclusion" or "representation" of the vignettes in this way is also, for me, a new provocation towards undoing. I am lost because of what I once thought I had found.

New Directions: Learning beyond the Arts

> [T]ake action together, to understand, to deal with the given problem that
> we share in common, [because alone] neither of us has the knowledge
> that's required to solve that problem. The knowledge itself is the product
> of our action.
>
> O'Neal, as cited in Hammer, 1992, p. 139

There are always limits to what one can understand, be, or realize. But together there is a level of possibility and potential that can be achieved when, through love, "visions of the heart" (Long & Dickason, 2011) can bloom. These visions of the heart have been described through the stories of the participants and through their engagements with the arts curriculum. These "projects of drama, are the projects of life" (Gallagher, 2000, p. 132) in which the "curriculum is a moving form. That is why we have trouble capturing it, fixing it in language, lodging it in our matrix … we are (always) trying to grasp a moving form, to catch it at the moment that it slides from being the figure, the object and goal of action" (Grumet, 1988). And isn't this the gift? As the curriculum moves, shapes, and reshapes itself, so do we. As our students grasp an understanding of something once beyond the limits of what they knew, we are all changed. The implications of these internal changes, however, must be reflected in the institutions and systems that we support. In relation to teacher agency, this research has exemplified how pre- and in-service teachers can engage with reconciliation through the arts curriculum. However, love also means creating spaces for a diversity of voices and experiences.

Sto:lo writer Lee Maracle is described as one of the most consistent and compelling truth-tellers writing today, who is as insistent on the important work Indigenous people must do within as she is on the work non-Indigenous peoples are called upon to undertake. Maracle has committed much of her work to telling hard truths with fierce love, as realized in this principle: "If you have hard truths to offer up to someone make sure the voice is soft, the language beautiful and that you protect the dignity of the other. When the storm clears, make sure you all see the sunshine" (Maracle, as cited in Justice, 2018, p. 160). This research has sought to concern itself with learning what "hard truths" individual pre- and in-service teachers need to learn about in order to feel confident enough to take the TRC's educational Calls for Action into their classrooms and to then share these truths through the arts. Through play-creation processes, they have risked, created, explored, and imagined what it means to live by the words of Lilla Watson, an Indigenous Australian visual artist: "If you have come here to help me, you are wasting your time. But if you have come here because your liberation is bound up with mine, then let us work together." Working together. Living together. Becoming a good ancestor. Living in a good way. These are some of the starting points that participants began with because "the responsibility rests with all of us to create space for Indigenous Knowledges and Worldviews in learning settings. We must all open our minds as well as our hearts to the different ways knowledge is constructed, shared, and valued if education is to benefit all students" (Hare, 2011, as cited in Long & Dickinson, 2011, p. 104). While the work of learning hard truths is challenging for the settler/newcomer, it is nothing compared to the challenge Indigenous people face, as Marie Battiste describes:

> Indigenous peoples worldwide are still undergoing trauma and stress from genocide and the destruction of their lives by colonization. Their stories are often silenced as they are made to endure other atrocities ... From them and for all Indigenous peoples worldwide, we seek to initiate dialogue, advance a postcolonial discourse, and work actively for a transformation of colonial thought. It becomes our greatest challenge and our honour to move beyond the analysis of naming the site of our oppression to act in individual and collective ways to effects change at many levels and to live in a good way. (Justice, 2018, p. 159)

Battiste reminds us of the ongoing and historical trauma and stress that colonization has caused but also that there is honour in rising to the challenge of living well and moving in a new direction, together. There is a focus on stepping together in a new direction. We must learn to work with(in) an ethic of care. We must learn more about racial equilibrium and how to remake racial hierarchies into productive spaces (Boghossian & Lindsay, 2019). Because, as Alayna Kolodziechuk reminds us, *This isn't over.* There is work to be done. There are hard truths to tell with fierce love, and the arts allow us to pick up where words cannot tread, plunging us into the depths of our being through the strongest of emotions towards connection and becoming. The arts help share hard truths, because there is a fundamental difference between how learning happens in the arts and what traditional assessment practices can capture in regard to what the arts teach/what learning is "shown." If "the most significant kind of learning in virtually any field creates a desire to pursue learning in that field when one doesn't have to, [then] the really important outcomes in education are located not within the school, but outside it ... [this means that the] aim of the educational process inside schools is not to finish something, but to start something. It is not to cover the curriculum, but to uncover it" (Eisner, 2002, p. 90). This shift in thinking about the purpose of education means that learning through the arts (i.e., how to foster relationships, dialogue with oneself and the other, listen, and develop heightened awareness and somatic knowledges) may never be measurable in a way that is useful to statisticians or policy makers who are mandated to write reports with deliverables and actionable items for standardized implementation. However, if the discourse around education shifts to focusing on a process of learning to create ourselves, then working together across domains to foster the learning that happens through the arts may be more readily recognized.

Coming Full Circle

Two young women, both in their twenties, sit cross-legged in a circle side by side at the end of the term. On this last day of class, Teresa and Arlene listen as each of their classmates speak about a challenge and joy they experienced in their drama education course. The person speaking holds a lit candle and when they finish reflecting, they pass the candle to the person on their right. This debriefing circle signifies what Tom Dearhouse calls "coming full circle" because when the last person speaks and the candle is blown out, each pre-service teacher will stand up and leave this circle in order to begin co-creating one of their own.

Sing the Brave Song: This Isn't Over!

WRITTEN BY ALAYNA KOLODZIECHUK

Front of House Opens

[Play house music, dimming lights just before "Cold" (0:00–2:48).]

[At 0:12 cast enters two by two from centre stage holding Google search results. Present to audience until exiting at end of "no longer exist" (2:10). Julianna and Julie exit stage left, Jesse and Asha exit stage right. Song continues to play; lights focus on pile of red dresses at centre downstage.]

[Possible projection of Google search images.]

Scene 1: Richard Niquay

[Julie enters at centre stage.]

JULIE: Richard, of Wemotaci First Nations reserve Quebec, said: "We must ensure that the things that happened are remembered. I wonder if Canadians really want to hear the truth."

[Julie exits at centre stage.]

Scene 2: Tracey Deere

[Julianna plays video: "When everything changed" (0:00–3:14 sec).]

Written for Dr. Mindy R. Carter, Department of Integrated Studies in Education, McGill University. Script: Fall 2016, revised 14 May 2017. Production: Spring 2017. Original cast: Julie Reckziegel, Julianna Astorino, Asha Bittenbender, Jesse Meredith.

Scene 3: We Start Here

[Jesse enters at stage right; Julianna enters at stage left.]

JESSE: Indigenous students in Canada have the highest drop-out, absenteeism, and adolescent suicide rates in the country.

JULIANNA: Many teacher education programs are investing heavily in resources and initiatives on Indigenous topics. However, most Quebec institutions have not to the same extent.

Part of this project is to bring Quebec Indigenous content and related issues of equity and diversity into the teacher education program at McGill using drama and theatre.

[Acknowledge each other.]

JESSE: In considering the issues facing Indigenous peoples in education, the impact of Canada's Indian Residential School system can't be ignored.

As a result of the residential schools, the educational experience of Indigenous children has been defined by policies intended to create long-lasting damage. Abuse and neglect of children in the schools was rampant, education poor.

Consider S.R. McVitty, Principal of Mount Elgin Industrial School, who said: "In the case of the Indian, a little learning is a dangerous thing."

JULIANNA: The purpose of the residential schools, it was said, was "to kill the Indian in the child."

JESSE: Canada's Truth and Reconciliation Commission was tasked with uncovering the truth about what happened during the residential school period. After collecting more than 7,000 statements from school survivors, the Commission made ninety-four Calls to Action to address the legacy of the residential schools and reconcile the broken relationship between Indigenous and non-Indigenous Canadians.

JULIANNA: The Commission says, "reconciliation is not an Aboriginal problem, it is a Canadian one."

We start here.

[Both step forward.]

They say time heals everything. That's a lie.

JESSE: They say it will take seven generations to fix what went on.

Scene 4: Priorities

[Julie and Asha enter from centre, bringing a table. Jesse and Julianna pick up chairs. Chatting.]

ASHA: I really hope this meeting ends before six.

[Asha, Jesse, Julianna immediately look bored.]

JULIE: And arising from the ninety-four Calls to Action from the Truth and Reconciliation Commission, many of which aim to limit educational gaps between Aboriginal and non-Aboriginal Canadians; to develop culturally appropriate curricula, and curricula that includes residential schools, treaties, and Aboriginal Peoples' contributions to Canada; and to promote reconciliation ... there is a motion before the board to adopt ...

JESSE: Excuse me, I'm sorry to interrupt you. No one here doesn't want to help the Aboriginals ...

But I know I speak for others when I say ... what about all the other parents here with kids who have their own issues that they're facing? How are we going to help them?

JULIANNA: My daughter has autism. Autistic students have always been left behind. On top of that, across the country there have been major cuts to funding for interventions and other treatments.

ASHA: What about the French-language issues that came up during our last meeting?

JESSE: What are we going to do about childhood obesity? We need to prioritize proper nutrition for students in schools!

JULIE: Of course, and thank you for raising all of these important issues, but one thing the motion before the Board mentions, as does the Truth and Reconciliation Report itself ...

JULIANNA: I just think we have to come back to the issue about the disabled kids in our schools.

JESSE: And what about cyber-bullying!

ASHA: Ya, and what's happening with new sex ed classes?

JULIE: Not to at all take away from any of these other very important issues. Everyone, please, hear me out. But as the Truth and Reconciliation Report found, the question of how we engage with Aboriginal issues in our education settings is a question of utmost urgency across the country. We are at a breaking point and are being told we have to prioritize these needs.

JULIANNA: What about the needs of all of our other students? Do those issues not need prioritizing?

JULIE: Yes of course. But they are saying we need to …

ASHA: I think we should table this discussion.

[Jesse then Asha exit stage right. Julianna exits stage left.]

JULIE: They are saying we have to prioritize these issues somehow. How are we going to do that?

Scene 5: The Context

[Asha and Jesse enter stage right. Julianna enters stage left.]

JULIANNA: Archaeologists say that Aboriginal people have lived in parts of Canada for 14,000 years.

ASHA: Prior to European contact, population estimates for Indigenous people living in North America range from 50 to 100 million. Since confederation, the population of Canada's Aboriginal peoples had decreased by 80 per cent.

JESSE: Today's First Nations population is estimated at 1.4 million.

JULIE: There are over 600 different groups in Canada, each with their own cultural and belief systems.

ASHA: There are over sixty First Nations languages in Canada.

JULIE: There are 2,400 reserves.

JESSE: Thirteen per cent of the Indigenous population in Canada is in Quebec.

JULIANNA: In Quebec, the Aboriginal languages most frequently reported as mother tongues were the Cree languages, Inuktitut, Innu/Montagnais and Atikamekw.

ASHA: McGill University sits on the traditional territory of the Kanien'kehá:ka people, otherwise known as the people of the Mohawk.

JULIE: The residential school period lasted 130 years. The closure of the last residential school was not until 1996.

JULIANNA: About 150,000 Indigenous children went through the residential school system.

JESSE: It could start with a knock on the door.
[Julianna knocks the floor with her foot. Julianna, Jesse, Asha step back.]

JULIE: "I was 8 years old. Somebody ran up to us and said, 'the police are here, your father wants you to go in the house.' We thought something had happened to my mother. At home, my mother was crying, and my father went outside. We were put in a vehicle and taken away ... they brought us to the train station without luggage, with only what we were wearing."
[Jesse steps forward.]

JESSE: "I could recognize those who attended residential schools ... There are parents who don't know how to love, how to show affection. There are some families of survivors who treat their children the way they were treated at school. For example, they all take their baths together with their underwear on."

JULIE: "The students were given numbers upon arrival at the school."
[Asha and Julianna step forward.]
"J'etais le numéro quatre-vingt sept."

ASHA: "I was fourteen, and then nineteen, and then six."

JULIANNA: "Je suis quarante trois."

JESSE: "Sixteen."

JULIANNA: Students suffered neglect and physical, sexual, and emotional abuse. The schools were structurally unfit and unsanitary. Tuberculosis was a major problem for decades at the schools. Some children tried to run away, to return to homes hundreds or even thousands of kilometres away, only to die in the elements.
The purpose of the residential schools, it was said, was "to kill the Indian in the child." There was family and community breakdown.

ASHA: The government and churches running the schools knew about the rampant abuse by the early 1800s. Complaints were ignored.

JULIANNA: Confirmed deaths at residential schools: 6,000. That means about one out of every twenty-three students died. Senator Murray Sinclair says that the real number may be five or even ten times higher, because records are so poor.

JULIE: Deaths without a listed name: thirty-two per cent.

ASHA: Deaths without a listed location: forty-three per cent.

JESSE: Deaths without a listed cause: forty-nine per cent.

After increasing pressure and court cases, in 2008, Stephen Harper issued a public apology to former students of Canada's residential school system, calling it a "sad chapter in our history."

JULIE: The prime minister was joined by the leaders of the other parties represented in the Canadian House of Commons. The Honourable Gilles Duceppe asked Canadians to: "picture a small village, a small community. Now picture all of its children, gone. No more children between seven and sixteen playing in the lanes or the woods, filling the hearts of their Elders with their laughter and joy."

ASHA: As for the churches, The Anglican, Presbyterian, and United Churches of Canada have also issued apologies for their involvement in the residential schools. Approximately seventy per cent of the schooling was done by the Catholic Church.

JULIE: The intergenerational effects of residential schooling and other discriminatory laws are still being understood.

JESSE: Incarceration rates: despite being only four per cent of the population, of those sentenced to time in custody, thirty-six per cent of women and twenty-five per cent of men are Indigenous. In some institutions, prisoner populations are as high as ninety per cent Indigenous. Indigenous people are ten times more likely to be incarcerated than other Canadians.

ASHA: In traditional Indigenous cultures, suicide didn't exist. Today, suicides and self-inflicted injuries rank as the leading cause of death for First Nations people younger than forty-four.

JESSE: In Attawapiskat, eleven people attempted suicide in one night. Twenty-eight in one month. 100 in a seven-month period.

JULIE: For 20 years, Pikangikum, a reserve in Ontario, has had – by far – the highest suicide rate in the world.

JULIANNA: For young First Nations women, the suicide rate is a staggering twenty-one times that of their non-Indigenous counterparts.

JULIE: Before European settlers came to Canada, it was not uncommon for Aboriginal women to hold equal power to men, including to take power away from the chief. Today, Indigenous women in Canada are five times more likely to die a violent death.

JULIANNA: The number of missing or murdered Indigenous women in Canada since 1980 is now over 4,000.

JULIE: The REDress Project involves hanging red dresses in trees throughout neighbourhoods.

JULIANNA: They just kind of blow in the wind, and it is just to show the fact that these women are gone and will never be able to come back.

Scene 6: These Women Are Gone and Will Never Be Able to Come Back

[Play: "Natural Blues" (0:00–5:00)]
[Julie, Jesse, Julianna exit stage right.]

ASHA: Where is she?
[Jesse, Julianna, and Julie enter stage right with various props at "Went down the hill" (0:53). Jesse and Julianna exit right after Asha approaches table. Julie exits stage left. Asha exits centre at end of song.]
[Julianna, Asha, Jesse, and Julie return from centre. All hang dresses in silence. Exit when finished: Asha and Jesse exit stage left. Julie and Julianna exit stage right.]

Scene 7: Teachable Moment: Micro-Aggressions

[Julianna enters stage right; Jesse enters stage left.]

JULIANNA: Students' experience of racism in schools comes predomi-
nantly from teachers.

[Julianna exit stage right.]

JESSE: So, he asked me this, and I'm honestly thinking ... I usually
skip this section because it's not all that important. I mean,
aren't there elective courses for that?

[Exit stage left.]

Scene 8: Cindy

[Julie enters stage right with Julianna carrying "Justice
#MMIWG" banner with Julie. Face banner to audience at centre
and lay it down. Julie joins Asha and Jesse at stage left exit. Projected images related to Cindy and her case throughout.]

JULIANNA: Donna MacLeod sat down with the Globe and Mail in spring of
2015 to discuss the aftermath of her daughter's death. Cindy
Gladue was thirty-six years old when she died, leaving behind three teenage daughters. She loved cooking shows and
was known for her ribs and apple crisp. She was witty. She
loved to draw.

Two days after Cindy was found, Bradley Barton was arrested
in connection with her death. During the murder trial, the
court was supposed to warn Donna about graphic images
of her daughter so she could avoid seeing them. One day,
without warning, a photo flashed onto a large screen in
the courtroom. The image of her daughter's naked, blood-
soaked body was forever burned into her brain. She died in
a bathtub, bleeding out from an eleven-centimetre vaginal
wound. There's no doubt that her last hours were horrific.

When she was found, reports indicate that the shower curtain
was red with blood. There was blood on the walls, the tile
floor, the sides of the toilet and smeared on the faucets. One
officer testified during the preliminary inquiry that blood
had "pooled over the side of the tub."

As for the accused, he claimed that the massive injury to Cindy
was a result of rough sex. He testified that he had his hand
inside her and when he pulled it out, he saw blood. He
asked if she was having her period. He refused to pay her,
washed up and went to bed. He said she then went to use

the washroom. He said he discovered her body later that morning. He then cleaned up the bathroom a little, prepared for work, and checked out of the hotel.

The Crown argued that he intentionally stabbed her. For the first time in Canadian history, the judge allowed a body part – Cindy's preserved vagina – to be presented as evidence at the trial. There it was, on a courtroom overhead projector. The Crown felt the jury had to see the nature of the injury: "This is not an accident," she said.

This move was seen by many as dehumanizing and a desecration of Cindy's body, an affront to her dignity. It did not have the effect on the jury that the Crown hoped for.

The jury was not told about the accused's search history on his laptop: pornography depicting "gaping vaginas and extreme penetration and torture." It was too prejudicial.

The jury of nine men and two women – none Native – deliberated for a day and a half.

[Asha, Julie, and Jesse enter from stage left.]

Ms. Foreperson, has the jury reached a verdict?

ASHA: Yes, Chief Justice. We are unanimous.

JULIANNA: In the charge of first degree murder, how do you find the accused?

ASHA: We find the accused not guilty.

JULIANNA: The jury didn't consider lesser charges such as manslaughter or even sexual assault.

[Asha, Julie, and Jesse exit stage left.]

Petitions, letter writing campaigns, and protests erupted across Canada. On the day of the protests in Cindy's honour, her thirteen-year-old daughter posted on Facebook: "How can I kill myself when I'm already dead."

The Crown appealed the decision which is currently being reviewed. If the appeal goes through, Donna says she is prepared to sit through another trial. For her daughter's sake. And she hopes that the Crown's case is successful this time.

The accused lives in Ontario with his common-law spouse of ten years.

Justice for Cindy Gladue. Justice for all missing and murdered women and girls.

Scene 9: White Tears?

[From backstage centre.]

JESSE:　　　I know some bad things happened, But I didn't have anything to do with it.

JULIANNA:　It's not really that bad, is it? I mean maybe it is, but whose fault is that, then?
　　　　　　[Julie and Asha enter stage left.]

JULIE:　　　I worked hard for what I have. Why can't they?

ASHA:　　　They already get free education and no taxes.

JESSE:　　　We all can't just have things handed to us.

JULIANNA:　The issues are just so big and so complex.

JULIE:　　　What can we do? I have no idea!

ASHA:　　　What about … listening … to what they have to say?

JESSE:　　　No.

ASHA:　　　Right. I mean how much more attention can we really give to this issue?

JESSE:　　　Ya ok, I hear what you're saying. You're right. But you have to admit … you're not like most of the rest of them.
　　　　　　[Exits left.]

JULIE:　　　I'm not a racist, but …
　　　　　　[Exits right.]

JULIANNA:　I have a friend who's Native!
　　　　　　[Exits right.]

ASHA:　　　I know some bad things happened. But that was a long time ago.
　　　　　　[Exits centre.]

Scene 10: Another Day, Another Story

[Jesse plays video for: multimedia montage of images, videos, twitter posts, newspaper headlines, statistics, commercials/ advertising practices, etc. collected demonstrating racism and

other forms of discrimination against Indigenous peoples living in Canada. Issues are current, many of which are expressly
rooted in the residential school experience.]

Scene 11: Teachable Moment: I Need Help with This

[Both enter right.]

JULIANNA: Can I ask you something? Why do First Nations live on
reserves?

JULIE: I don't know. We could google it.

[Exits stage centre.]

Scene 12: Peggy Formsma

[Asha enters stage left.]

ASHA: Earlier this year, Peggy Formsma of Attawpiskat said: "People
portray the negative stuff, what about the beauty? What
about the resilience? What we came through? We're still
here. We're still here. And we are a strong people."

[Asha exits stage left.]

Scene 13: Phil Fontaine

[Jesse enters from centre.]

JESSE: We have talked a lot about how far Canada still has to go to
understand, acknowledge, and repair the wrongdoings committed against Indigenous Canadians.

We also want to talk about how far we have come. Not because
we need to feel complacent, that we have come far enough –
no, we don't need that.

In 1990, Phil Fontaine, then Grand Chief of the Assembly of
Manitoba Chiefs, spoke publicly about the abuse that he experienced at residential school: "In my grade three class" he
said, "if there were twenty boys, every single one of them ...
would have experienced what I experienced." This was the
first time the issue had been vocalized, out loud, in a public
setting. It put the issue on the national agenda.

Phil Fontaine was the lead complainant in a multibillion dollar
lawsuit that put the physical, sexual, and psychological abuse

he suffered at residential school front and centre. He was integral in encouraging others to come forward.

Within 10 years, more than 8,500 residential school survivors had initiated lawsuits. Not only were these lawsuits costly, lengthy, and legally complex, but the odds were stacked against the claimants. During this time, there are no reported decisions where the court believed the residential school plaintiff over an alleged perpetrator, except where the perpetrator was already a known sexual predator. They had to defend their experiences in a system that did not yet recognize the loss of language, family, and culture central to the residential school experience.

Faced by growing lawsuits, the federal government, provinces, and churches agreed to enter into a settlement agreement process.

The successful negotiation of the Settlement Agreement in 2005 – the largest and most expansive agreement in Canadian history – meant the resolution of more than 20 class actions and more than 15,000 individual claims relating to the 130-year period of injustices.

The Settlement Agreement and the formal apology by Prime Minister Stephen Harper represent the culmination of years of political struggle, changes in societal attitudes, court decisions, and immense pressure to negotiate. Through it all, survivors kept the issue alive.

This monumental achievement through adversity is truly unprecedented in Canadian history. This monumental achievement is something we should all be proud of.

One year ago, on the McGill campus, Phil Fontaine said: "But I'd be lying to you, I'd be trying to fool you, if I were to suggest that somehow I am a whole person and I've healed myself … I'm not, I'm not, I just am not. But I'm strong enough not to feel the shame I carried with me, strong enough not to be burdened by the guilt that was such a huge part of my life."

Scene 14: Teachable Moment: Ask the Hard Questions

[Jesse picks up chair. Asha enters from stage left with chair, Julie and Julianna enter from stage right with chairs.]

| JULIE: | At the end of last class, we were talking about the Canada 150 events happening this summer. Vancouver's events are called "Canada 150+ moving forward together." I wanted to make sure we talked about why this is significant. Let's think back to our unit on Indigenous peoples in Canada for a second. Why might "150+" be an important distinction to make to the Canada 150? |

Scene 15: Sing the Brave Song

JULIE:	What is reconciliation?
ASHA:	Lilla Watson said: "If you have come here to help me, you are wasting your time. But if you have come here because your liberation is bound up with mine, then let us work together."
JESSE:	We recognize that we are gathered today on the traditional territory of the Kanien'kehá:ka people, and that this land is subject to the Two Row Wampum Treaty.
ASHA:	Reconciliation.
JULIANNA:	What does "reconciliation" mean?
JULIE:	Acceptance. Understanding. Knowing the truth. Building trust.
ASHA:	Respect for Indigenous Canadians. We are all Treaty people.
JESSE:	We need to be learning more about these issues in school.
JULIANNA:	Be brave. This matters to me.
ASHA:	Some things they say will help with reconciliation:
JULIE:	Listening.
JESSE:	Any reconciliation with the Indigenous people in Canada will have to include reconciliation with the environment.
JULIE:	Public education. Being able to ask questions. I don't think people really know what happened at all.
ASHA:	Think of all these parents that have lost children. It's not right.
JULIANNA:	I want to be supportive. I'm sorry for the things that have been going on. I don't want them to go on anymore.

ALL: I'm sorry for the things that have been going on.

ASHA: Don't say you're sorry. I think it's really our job to listen. Native people always end up compromising.

JULIANNA: Now is the time for action.

JESSE: We have to just do right by each other. Honour the treaties. This month, Canada finally removed its objector status to the UN Declaration on the Rights of Indigenous Peoples.

JULIE: Ensure the full implementation of the declaration.

JULIANNA: On our last count, 556 memoirs and anthologies by residential school survivors have been published. We should read them.

JULIE: We must take responsibility for the current gap between the educational success of Aboriginal and non-Aboriginal Canadians.

JULIANNA: Despite being subjected to aggressive assimilation policies for nearly 200 years, Aboriginal people have maintained their identity and their communities. That is worth celebrating.

ASHA: Buy from First Nations businesses. Support Indigenous artists. Make art together.

JULIE: Don't be afraid to question things. Notice things. The words we use. The names we use.

JULIANNA: Many places in Canada are reconsidering the use of certain names and symbols in light of reconciliation.

JESSE: Vancouver city council moved to consider using First Nations names for everything from buildings to parks.

ASHA: What about the McGill Redmen?

JULIANNA: Be mindful. Be respectful.

JULIE: Don't let this be the end. This isn't over.
          [Exit.]

Reconciliation!

WRITTEN BY JENNIFER HAYDEN-BENN AND THE GRADE FIVE AND SIX STUDENTS OF ST. EDMUND'S SCHOOL (2018–19)

Script

Throughout the show, the six main characters (two Elders and four kids), are located on the front stage. The Elders are teaching the children about their history and culture through stories. During each scene, when a story starts, the spotlight pans to the back stage where you see the story play out with other actors. Sometimes they are speaking roles, sometimes non-speaking. Kid 4 starts the show out with a bad attitude, but over the course of the stories, develops a greater appreciation of her culture and history.

Scene 1: Creation Story/Turtle Island (5ML)

Backstage: Image of Tree of Life & clouds, then birds flying, then Turtle Island
Props: Tortoise sandbox covered with blue fabric representing water, Sky Woman and Sky Chief standing on a piece of stage.
Actors: six mains, Sky Woman & Sky Chief (non-speaking role)
Song: Carry It On by Buffy Sainte-Marie

> *[Children are playing with wooden canoes and wooden toys. Elders are at a campfire.]*

ELDER 1:   Children, gather round. It's time for storytelling.
            [Children gather around excitedly.]

KID 1:   Ooh, I love storytelling.

KID 2:   [To Grandfather (Elder 1)]
            What's the story about today?

ELDER 2:   Well, let's start at the beginning with the story of Creation.
                Then you'll know where our land came from, the amazing
                Turtle Island.

KID 3:   That's exciting! Let's get started.

KID 4:   [groaning]
                This is so boring, let's just get it over with.

ELDER 1:   Storytelling is such an important part of our culture. I know
                in time, you will come to appreciate it.

ELDER 2:   In the beginning, in the world we know now, there was no
                land. Only water and creatures of the sea. But up above,
                there was a place called Karonhiak:ke (Ga-roo-nya:Gé),
                The Sky World.

ELDER 1:   The beings who lived in Sky World were much like us, but
                with more strength and powers. One day, Sky Woman
                wanted seeds from the root of the Tree of Life.

ELDER 2:   As she and her husband, Sky Chief, were digging the roots,
                suddenly, the tree fell through the ground. Sky Woman
                went through the hole and started falling toward the wa-
                ters below.

KID 1:   Oh, my goodness! What happened to her?

KID 2:   Seriously, what a cliff-hanger!

ELDER 1:   You must listen children, we will continue. A flock of birds
                came to her rescue. She landed on their backs.

ELDER 2:   As they tried to bring her back up to Sky World, they quickly
                realized she was too heavy. As they lowered her down gen-
                tly, a kind turtle lent his back for her to land on.

ELDER 1:   While she was falling, she grabbed some of the seeds from
                the Tree of Life. As she danced on the back of the turtle
                and sprinkled the seeds, the turtle's back grew and grew.
                Some of these plants included tobacco and strawberry
                seeds.

KID 4:   [sarcastically]
                Oh my, this is an epic tale.

KID 3:   The turtle's back grew? Is that Turtle Island?

ELDER 2:   Yes, my dear. That is the story of how our land, Turtle Island, came to be. Today it is known as North America.

Scene 2: Mother Earth (5 ML)

Backstage: Image of nature (i.e., forest with different animals)
Props: Bows/arrows for hunters
Actors: Two hunters, group of four to five Indigenous people in a community (non-speaking roles)
Song: Seasons by Indian City

KID 1:   What a beautiful story and such a beautiful song!

KID 4:   [playing on iPad]
Sorry, what did you say?

KID 2:   Come on, you need to put your iPad away! You're going to miss so much!

KID 3:   Seriously! I loved the story of Sky Woman and Mother Earth. We have so much to be thankful for, with all that Mother Earth provides for us.

ELDER 1:   I'm so glad you all realize how fortunate we are to receive such gifts from the Mother Earth. We must always protect her, and never take more than we need.
[Spotlight pans to back of stage.]

HUNTER 1:   [speaking to a group of Indigenous people]
We are just back from the annual moose hunt.

HUNTER 2:   As always, the moose we hunted chose us because we hunt with love and respect in our hearts, and we share with those in need.

HUNTER 1:   We are so fortunate with what the Creator has provided for us.

HUNTER 2:   Yes, we must make sure we always demonstrate ceremony, honour, and respect for what we receive. We must always be thankful and have gratitude.
[Spotlight pans to front of stage.]

ELDER 2:   The tradition of moose-hunting has been passed down for generations. We have to make sure we always maintain the

balance of our ecosystem and use all of the parts of the
animals that we hunt.

KID 1:   Is that why we use animal skins to create our clothing?

ELDER 1:   That is right. We use all of the parts of the animals we hunt
                for food, warmth, clothing and tools. We must always be
                thankful.

Scene 3: Culture (6AE)

Backstage: Totem poles, four-colour symbol
Props: Totem pole, two rattles
Actors: Six mains, two Mohawk people, two Haida people (who are
learning about each other's traditions)
Song: Quand le jour se lève

KID 1:   All this talk of nature reminds me of the traditional clothing
                I see at the Powwow every summer.

KID 2:   Yeah, and the beautiful totem poles we saw at the museum.

ELDER 1:   Totem poles are a wonderful tradition of our brothers and
                sisters that are Haida. Did you know that totem poles are
                not meant to be brought inside?

                [Spotlight pans to back of stage, where there is a totem pole
                and 4 people dressed in traditional clothing. Two are Mohawk,
                two are Haida.]

MOHAWK 1:   [admiring totem pole]

                I've always admired these beautiful totem poles. It is not
                something that is part of our tradition.

MOHAWK 2:   It's true. Can you tell us a bit about the totem pole tradition?

HAIDA 1:   Of course! It would be our pleasure.

HAIDA 2:   A totem pole is usually read from the bottom up, with the
                bottom being the position of the most importance.

HAIDA 1:   Yes, the bottom symbol is the most visible and prominent, so
                therefore, the most important.

MOHAWK 1:   That makes sense. So, what do these beautiful symbols
                mean?

HAIDA **2:**   On this totem pole, we see a killer whale. This represents family, since whales raise their children with care. He is also said to protect those who travel far from home.

MOHAWK **2:**   [pointing to Eagle]

And what about this one?

HAIDA **1:**   The eagle is very important and is known as the "master of skies." He is known to have the closest relationship to the Creator. He is said to be a messenger to the Creator.

MOHAWK **1:**   We use eagle feathers a great deal at home too.

HAIDA **2:**   I see that you are wearing four colours on your clothing. Do they have any special meaning?

MOHAWK **2:**   As a matter of fact, yes, they do. These are the colours of the medicine wheel. They represent many things: emotions, direction, and all of the races of humanity. Each people have their own customs, language and way of life, and we must have respect for all.

[Spotlight pans back to front stage.]

KID **1:**   That is all so interesting.

KID **2:**   It's so exciting, almost makes me want to dance!

KID **4:**   I'd rather just play on my iPad.

KID **3:**   Come on man, let's listen.

ELDER **1:**   Speaking of dance, we have so many traditional dances.

[Spotlight pans to back of stage.]

[Grade 6 Alligator Dance on backstage, Mohawk 1 and 2 play rattles]

KID **4:**   [enters scene on top part of stage after dance]

Hey, what are these cool rattles? And what was that dance about?

MOHAWK **1:**   That was the Alligator Dance, a traditional social dance for the Iroquois. Would you like to try to play the rattle?

[Start song, Kid 4 plays rattle during song, then returns to front stage.]

Scene 4: Loss (5NM)

Backstage: picture of first contact, cold northern scene, De Beers/Atta-wapiskat on news, protests
Props: blanket
Actors: Six mains, two settlers (meant to be like Gaston/Lefou characters from Beauty and the Beast), two Indigenous people, one Indigenous Chief, two news reporters
Song: Tiny Hands by Quantum Tangle

KID **1:**   That was really amazing! It reminds me of watching the Elders dance at the Powwow last summer.

ELDER **1:**   Yes, we have such talent among our people. Our traditions of old are still alive and well today.

KID **2:**   There is so much to celebrate: creation, Mother Earth, Sky Woman, Turtle Island, our songs, music and dance. Wow!

KID **4:**   I must admit, that instrument and dance were pretty cool. Thinking I should jet soon though, so I have some iPad time!

KID **3:**   All the stories so far have such happy endings. Do you have any stories that don't end so well?

KID **4:**   Now that could be something interesting ... maybe I'll stick around for a while.

ELDER **2:**   Let me tell you about what happened to our land ...
               [Spotlight pans to the top stage. Three Indigenous people off to side of stage talking in a circle. Two settlers approach.]

SETTLER **1:**   Look at all of this beautiful land!

SETTLER **2:**   Hey, wait! There's people here. Who are those people?
                [Settlers approach the group; Indigenous people turn toward them.]

SETTLER **1:**   Hello. Do you live here?

SETTLER **2:**   Yeah, yeah, do you live here? Is this your land?

CHIEF: Whoa! Slow down. We live here, but the land is not ours. We belong to this land. Our ancestors have been here for thousands of years. We'd like to welcome you. Come over here, we'll show you how we live.

[Spotlight pans to front of stage.]

ELDER **1**: When Europeans first came, they had much to learn. We taught them how to fish, hunt, and which plants were medicine, and which were poisonous.

ELDER **2**: We traded our furs and medicines for items like weapons and spices. Things seemed to be going well.......
UNTIL

[Spotlight pans to back stage where settlers are speaking in hushed tones.]

SETTLER **1**: We need to tell the King about all this land. We need to take control. This land shall be ours.

SETTLER **2**: Yes, yes, tell the King. Tell the King. This land SHALL be ours.

SETTLER **1**: Indeed. We need a plan. More of us, less of them.

[Spotlight pans to front stage.]

ELDER **1**: Slowly, over time, the Europeans took our land. We had less and less space and were forced from our homes.

KID **4**: That's awful. How?

ELDER **2**: Many of us were made to move far north, to a land we weren't familiar with. We weren't used to it, and treacherous winter conditions made it hard to survive.

ELDER **1**: Diseases like smallpox and tuberculosis were brought over from Europe.

Sometimes, these diseases were spread intentionally among our people.

[Spotlight pans to back of stage. Settler 1 coughing on blanket in the background.

Three Indigenous people are off to the side talking.]

SETTLER **1**: We brought you some supplies.

INDIGENOUS **1**: That is helpful. Thank you very much.

SETTLER **2**: [nudging Settler 1 discreetly]
Of course, that's right. These will definitely help.

INDIGENOUS **2**: So many of our people are becoming sick.

SETTLER **1:**   [nudges back, coughs in blanket again, hands blankets to the Chief.
Spotlight pans to the front of stage.]

KID **1:**   Do you mean that these diseases were given to our people on purpose?

ELDER **2:**   Sadly, yes, that happened in many cases.

KID **4:**   Whoa, seriously?! That really is a terrible ending.

ELDER **1:**   Over time, we worked to get along with the settlers. Treaties were signed between our people and the Crown. In these agreements, we agreed to share some of our ancestral land and resources in exchange for various payments and promises.

ELDER **2:**   Our grandfathers and grandmothers signed these treaties, not just for themselves, but for seven generations ahead, including all of you. For our people, they were considered a sacred agreement between nations.

KID **3:**   This sounds promising. Negotiating is always helpful for us kids at recess.

ELDER **1:**   It did sound promising at the beginning. However, we've seen many situations where the treaties were forgotten as soon as money and valuable resources came into play.
[Spotlight pans to the back of stage, where a news reporter is at a desk reporting.]

REPORTER **1:**   Good evening folks. First tonight, we have another tragic story of Indigenous treaties being forgotten here in Canada. Recently, South African mining giant, De Beers, has decided to develop Ontario's first diamond mine in Attawapiskat.

REPORTER **2:**   That's right _____(name), people living in the Attawapiskat First Nation have held many protests recently as their traditional hunting grounds are being dug up in search of diamonds.

REPORTER **1:**   Yes _____, behind us you see a picture of one of those protests. De Beers arrived in Attawapiskat just after the news that their elementary school had been contaminated by 150,000 litres of diesel that had leaked into the substructure.

REPORTER **2**:	A lack of clean drinking water and proper shelter plague the community where De Beers has set up shop. The challenges are many for these folks, that is for sure.

Scene 5: Residential Schools (5LP)

Backstage: Pot cooking on an open fire, image of residential school, image of boy before and after entering residential school (drastic change in hair/clothing is so powerful)
Props: table with four chairs, scissors
Actors: 6 mains, Shin-Che, Shi She Etko, Mom, Dad, two teachers
Song: Stronger than Gold (Maria & Addison's composition)

ELDER **1**:	As you can see, our people have experienced great injustices and loss for many years. Loss of land, breaking of treaties, and spreading of diseases are only a few.
KID **1**:	Are there any other losses like these? Were children affected?
ELDER **2**:	Children were impacted in many ways. Perhaps the most tragic was when our children were forced to leave their families at a young age to go to residential schools.
KID **2**:	What is a residential school?
ELDER **1**:	Well, let me tell you. This is how it happened.
	[Spotlight moves to top stage. Mom, Dad, two children sitting at a dinner table.]
DAD:	Thank you Mother Earth for these gifts.
MOM:	We are so thankful for this delicious dinner of elk and vegetables.
SHIN CHE:	This food really is yummy!
SHI SHI ETKO:	Yes, thank you. And what do we have planned for tomorrow? Can we go to the river? Maybe go fishing and canoeing?
	[Mother and father look at each other sadly.]
FATHER:	Well …
	[sighs]
SHIN CHE:	What's wrong? Why do you look so sad?

MOTHER:	Tomorrow, you are both being picked up to go to residential school. We are sad because we won't see you until the salmon return to the river.
FATHER:	Yes, it is September now, and we won't see you until June.
SHI SHI ETKO:	But why do we have to go?
FATHER:	We miss you so much when you go, but we have no choice. It is the laws that make it so.
	[Shin Che and Shi shi etko look sad and squeeze each other's hands over the table.]
MOTHER:	Alright little ones, let's go and have storytime before bed.
	[Spotlight pans to the front stage. Crew sets up residential school background.]
ELDER 2:	As you can see, parents and children had no choice. They were forced to send their children far away to residential schools for many months at a time.
ELDER 1:	If parents refused, they could be arrested. Indian agents picked up the children on the reserves and they travelled by cattle truck, sometimes hundreds of kilometres from their homes.
	[Spotlight pans to top stage where residential school scene is set up.]
SHIN CHE:	This building and that lady look so scary.
SHI SHI ETKO:	Don't worry my Shin Che, we'll be home again soon. Just remember you can't speak our language or talk to me until we go back home.
SHIN CHE:	Can you stay with me?
TEACHER 1:	[yelling and splitting them up] Boys on this side, girls over here. There are some rules you need to understand while you are here.
TEACHER 2:	You must speak English or French. Boys and girls must never speak to each other. You will all be given jobs. Boys will garden and do carpentry. Girls will cook and clean.

TEACHER 1:	Once you enter, you will receive your new name, your number and your uniform. This is how you'll be known. [Students start to walk into the school.]
SHIN CHE:	[calls out] Shi shi etko no! I'll miss you!
TEACHER 2:	[points to Shin Che angrily] You, over here immediately. You can't follow the rules. [takes out scissors from pocket] It's time for your hair cut. [Spotlight pans to front of stage.]
ELDER 2:	At the schools, our children were often mistreated, had little food, and were forced to speak languages they didn't understand. Their long hair was cut, their clothes were changed, and they were not allowed to speak to their siblings.
ELDER 1:	It was an attempt to erase our culture. When the children went home, often, they were unrecognizable. They looked and sounded totally different. They prayed in ways their parents had never taught them to. But we are a strong people, and our culture survived.
ELDER 2:	Some parents never saw their children again. Many children – some 6000 – died in residential schools. Many parents were never told what happened to them. Those children are now buried in unmarked graves, cut off from their families.

Scene 6: Standing Up (6LL)

Actors: 6 mains
Song: Dreamchild by St. Willibrord School

KID 3:	Wow, I can't believe that happened to our people. When did the last residential school in Canada close?
ELDER 1:	It's hard to believe, but the last school only closed in 1996.
KID 1:	That was not very long ago.

ELDER 2:	It really wasn't. Our people are still trying to get over what happened and are still living with the many scars created by residential schools.
KID 4:	That's terrible. Did anyone take responsibility or apologize to our people? [said angrily]
ELDER 1:	Yes, after many years, the Government of Canada finally apologized for residential schools. Sadly, an apology does not erase the many wrongs that have been done.
KID 2:	You always say that actions speak louder than words. Did the government actually DO anything?
ELDER 2:	Yes, the government started a Truth and Reconciliation Commission. They investigated Indigenous history and residential schools. The stories of students who gave testament will be archived so future generations can learn from them.
ELDER 1:	The Commission has created a list of ways Canadians can move forward and begin reconciliation with us.
KID 3:	Wow, we've learned so much through these stories today.
KID 4:	We have. I'm really sorry I wasn't very cooperative earlier.
KID 1:	That's OK, everyone makes mistakes. Why haven't we learned much about all of this in school?
ELDER 2:	That's one of the recommendations of the Commission. That our children, Indigenous and non-Indigenous alike, learn the history of our land and our people.
KID 2:	It's so important that you taught us all of this, and it's sad that not many people know what happened.
KID 1:	It's so important that we learn so that nothing like this ever happens again.
ELDER 1:	Luckily, more and more people are finding out about both the positive and the dark sides of our history.
ELDER 2:	It's true, every single year, we see more and more of our non-Indigenous friends coming to celebrate at the Powwow.

ELDER **1:**   Speaking of Powwow, we have one planned for tonight! I hope you can all come. The dance you are about to see is a mix of traditional Powwow dance and hip hop moves. Like everyone, we are always changing and evolving, adopting new ideas along the way.

[Grade 6 Electric Powwow Dance]

ELDER **2:**   As we finish up this special time of storytelling, there is one last lesson that we'd like to leave you with.

ELDER **1:**   Perhaps one of the most important of all. It is through you, our youth, that real change can come. Your actions and words can raise awareness and bring together people from all backgrounds.

ELDER **2:**   Just look at this beautiful song created by students of St. Willibrord in Chateauguay. The students combine English, French, and Mohawk languages to convey a powerful message of unity, love, and respect for all.

Monologue: *I'm Still Canadian, Dad!*

WRITTEN BY MINDY R. CARTER

My dad is so Canadian. So, you know, lovely.

He has always been kind and gentle and sees the world in this "do unto your neighbour as you would have them do unto you" kind of attitude. I mean, he opens doors for women and makes me walk on the inside of the pavement, so I won't get splashed by a car driving by if the pavement is wet. For him being Canadian means working hard, spending time with your family, and enjoying the simple things in life, like fishing in the summer and telling stories at a bonfire by the lake. Him and my mom have been married 40 years this fall, and they met in high school in the same small town that my great-grandparents came to as immigrants over 100 years ago. His father was in the Second World War and so my dad has always respected the whole legacy of what that means to this country. How his father fought for freedom and we need to keep our appreciation for the sacrifice of others alive in our collective consciousness. He cares. He really does.

[CHUCKLES.]

Do you remember those "I am Canadian" commercials in the '90s? So, my brother, mom, and I happened to be watching one of them at the same time when they first came out and then just as the rant "aboot" Canadians being peacekeepers and not Americans "policing" the world

Performed for the Artful Inquiry Research Group Symposium, Fall 2020.

began, my dad walked in holding a Molson beer and wearing a plaid flannel shirt. Seriously!

We couldn't stop laughing! When my dad asked "what" we were sent off into hysterics again. It was too perfect – and I guess that's why I think of my dad as "so Canadian."

So honestly, I grew up in this great environment and family that has always just felt like the typical Canadian experience.

But then I moved away to go to school, and I was just, you know, exposed to different ideas and people and perspectives. I don't know when it happened exactly, but I was really interested in social justice issues and starting to get involved in student government to try and improve things. I became just more hyper aware about so many things, but especially about what narratives were missing in the collective Canadian conversation. I remember Kim Campbell was asked, like to explain Canada's history to the rest of the world in "Being Canadian" (2015) and she just said "Unknown." I even remember reading a book called *The Brief History of Canada* and in the introduction the first question asked was: What is Canada? What is a Canadian?

Here I was thinking: You want to know what a Canadian is, well, meet my dad! My dad is SO Canadian, end of story. But then the book talked about this ongoing debate about how trying to answer these questions has led to political, intellectual, religious, and media-related debates. Some nationalists suggested that we were a satellite of the US, while others argued for a break from the French and English colonial legacies. Around the same time, I remember reading a completely different take on the whole conversation by Leroy Little Bear. Bear called Canada a "Pretend Nation" that has a costume trunk beside it because it so quickly puts on the appropriate costume needed at a particular time in history to appear in a certain way to others. This is contrasted to the Native way of thinking that he describes as a "symbiosis that developed between the land, the environment, and ecological aspects." It was about that relationship that affects knowledge and the embodied identities of people through stories, beliefs, and metaphysics. Bear concludes:

So, if we look at Canada, it is not much different than a multibillionaire whose wealth is strictly on paper. It is not connected to the land. *It's like the person originally from San Francisco or Seattle, who then lived in Calgary for fifty or sixty years, and somebody asks, "Where are you from?" After fifty or sixty years of living in Calgary, the person answers, "I'm from San Francisco." Identity is being drawn elsewhere. So, it seems to me that if Canada were to be a true nation, it's going to have to embody the knowledge that has always been here. It's going to have to acknowledge its Aboriginal roots. Canada may have a constitution. Canada may have a government. Canada may have a legal system. But, just like that multibillionaire whose wealth exists entirely on paper, all of the above are simply a paper existence – not substantive in any sense. It doesn't arise from a mutual relationship with the totality of the ecology of territory.*

[Pause.]

I know.

It kind of changes everything, right?

How would you explain that idea of "being Canadian" to my dad?

*Fast-for*ward to being involved in this play – *Sing the Brave Song: This Isn't Over!* – and here I am looking at Indigenous issues framed through the lens of reconciliation – another, arguably, nationalistic construct. A lot of people have a lot of problems with this whole idea of "reconciliation."

Hey, no … don't get me wrong, I don't want to diminish the fact that in the production there are a lot of tough things that are explored and presented. One that comes to mind for me is the relationship between the police and Indigenous people – especially the lack of involvement by the police in relation to the missing and murdered Indigenous women and girls. But, I have police in my family and my parents are coming to see the show and so I am wondering if I should warn them about some things or something. There are just all these tensions in moving between these evolving world views. But at least we're trying to understand some of these things …

But, well, so I start to doubt myself and question, well, EVERYTHING. And I ask myself, OK, so what would I warn them about? What exactly? Wouldn't that just be another way of playing into these ideas of white fragility, where we don't want to hurt white people's feelings? I know some of my aunts and uncles are always saying:

"They just need to get over the past and move on. They've gotten enough money and you know what? I work harder than they do, and no one gives me anything."

[Looking at the audience]

I know, you're thinking who says that? But it's true.

Maybe I have to warn everyone else about my family.

Glossary

According to Joseph (2018), **Aboriginal** is used to indicate the collective group of people in Canada who "hold various rights and obligations under provision of the Indian Act and Section 35 of the 1903 Constitution Act" (p. 12).

Ally or **in Solidarity** is a member of an oppressor group who works to end a form of oppression which gives him or her an unearned privilege. "Becoming an ally means learning about systems of oppression, figuring out our own (conscious or unconscious) roles in maintaining those systems and then working alongside those most affected to try and address the inequity" (Bishop, 2014).

Appropriation is when an individual takes an artefact and makes it their own. It is "the act of taking possession of, or assigning purpose to, properties or ideas" (Esteban-Guitart, 2014).

Devised Theatre, frequently called collective creation, is a method of theatre-making in which "the whole creative team develops a show collaboratively. From actors to technicians, everyone is involved in the creative process."

Embodiment is a concept emphasizing the reciprocal relationship between mind (cognition, emotion) and body (motor behaviour, nonverbal behaviour, physiological processes). In introducing the concept of embodiment, Merleau-Ponty (1996) wrote: "to be a consciousness or rather *to be an experience* is to hold inner communication with the world, the body and other people, to be with them instead of being beside them" (p. 96).

First Nation came into usage as the replacement for "terms such as Indian and Native, which were in common usage at the time (in the

---

Ying (Elaine) Syuan Huang, GRA, assisted in compiling some of the terms in this glossary.

1970s) … and gradually became adopted by the general Canadian population (in the 1990s)" (Younging, 2018, p. 63). The term "First Nation" refers to a segment of the Indigenous Peoples in Canada, so if for example, one is referring to all Indigenous people in Canada (including Inuit and Metis) one would not use the term "First Nation."

Forgiveness is the emotional, mental, and spiritual process of letting go of resentment, indignation, or anger against another person for a perceived offence, difference, or mistake. Over the past quarter century, the concept of **political forgiveness** emerged to describe "the many recent governmental efforts to apologize and seek to atone for such large-scale historical wrongs as slavery, official systems of racial segregation, the dispossession of Indigenous populations of their lands and cultural heritage, campaigns of ethnic cleansing, and other instances of global injustice" (Hughes, 2011).

Image Theatre is a series of techniques that allow people to communicate through images and spaces, and not through words alone (Boal, 1979). It is a technique of the Theatre of the Oppressed in which a group of people sculpt their own or each other's bodies to express attitudes and emotions towards a given theme, such as bullying. They do this by individually stepping into the centre of a circle and remaking their still image to create tableaux – a vivid graphic scene of a group of people arranged as in a painting or sculpture. Because the sculptor should not speak while they shape the other participants, this allows for participants' reflection and exploration of different kinds of imbalances in power.

Improvisation is the act of inventing or executing something without planning and preparation.

Indian is used when citing the Indian Act of 1876 in a particular legal and historical context in relation to settlers' policies, treatment, and relationships with the Indigenous Peoples in the country that is now called Canada. "Indian [is not a term that is] otherwise use[d] unless in reference to a community that has made that choice for their name" (Joseph, 2018, p. 19). In Joseph's (2018) book *21 Things You May Not Know about the Indian Act*, he discusses how "Indian" was defined in the 1876 Indian Act as follows: "Any male person of Indian blood reported to belong to a particular band; Any child of such person; Any woman who is lawfully married to such a person" (p. 11); he also explains how this definition changed in the updated 1951 revision of the Indian Act to "A person who is pursuant to this Act is registered as an Indian" (p.11). For Gregory Younging (2018) in *Elements of Indigenous Style*, "Indian" is an inappropriate term used to describe the hundreds of distinct nations of Indigenous Peoples throughout North, Central, and South America and the Caribbean. It traces back to the explorer tradition and was coined by Columbus as he was "looking for Asia ... (He was) going to find India ... And so (he) looked at the first peoples ... on the shores and said, these must be Indians." The term, therefore, was a misnomer from the start, although it was widely used by explorers and missionaries ... Canadian federal government documents, and Canadian and American mainstream society up to the present day ... Avoid this term as a general descriptor of identity ... It is appropriate to use *Indian* to refer to the status of individual people under the Indian Act. In these situations, it is better to say *Status Indian*, or even *Status Indian under the Indian Act*, to clarify the specific context of use (p. 57).

Indian Day Schools or **Federal Indian Day Schools** were compulsory schools funded, managed, and controlled by the Federal Government of Canada and churches to assimilate Indigenous children into Euro-Canadian society. Unlike residential schools, which removed children from their families and communities, Indian day schools did not board students overnight. Since the 1920, close to 200,000 Indigenous children attended the Indian Day Schools. "By 1900 there were some 226 federally funded day schools in Indian reserves; the majority of teachers were missionaries, and the curriculum included a large proportion of religious instruction" (Miller, 1999, p. 1582). Many students who attended these schools experienced trauma associated with cultural harms, and in some cases, physical and sexual abuse at the hands of individuals entrusted with their care (Crown-Indigenous Relations and Northern Affairs Canada, 2018).

Indian Residential School (IRS) is an extensive school system set up by the Government of Canada and administered by churches to assimilate Indigenous children into Euro-Canadian culture. See also Residential schools.

Indigenous is the term the federal government of Canada used to replace "Aboriginal" in government communications in 2016. Some have argued that this was a "giant step back" because it reifies a nation-to-nation relationship between "Indigenous" and "Non-Indigenous" people in Canada (Joseph, 2018). The term Indigenous refers to the people who are indigenous to a place/land, and in Canada this is a collective term for "First Nation, Inuit, Metis" (Joseph, 2018, p.12). In the 2016 Census (Statistics Canada), over 1.6 million people in Canada identified as Indigenous, making up 4.9 per cent of the national population (Parrott, 2007).

Missing and Murdered Indigenous Women and Girls (MMIWG) is
a human rights crisis affecting Indigenous people in Canada and
the United States, including First Nations, Inuit, Metis, and Native
American communities. It refers to the issue of high and disproportionate rates of violence and the appalling numbers of missing and
murdered Indigenous women and girls in Canada and the United
States. In 2015, the Truth and Reconciliation Commission of Canada
supported the call for a national public enquiry into the disproportionate victimization of Indigenous women and girls. The National
Inquiry's Final Report was completed and presented to the public on
3 June 2019.

Monologue means an extended speech by one person in drama and
literature.

Quebec Education Plan (QEP) is a document published by Quebec's
Ministère de l'Éducation et de l'Enseignement supérieur (the Ministry of Education, Leisure, and Sports) to detail the essential knowledges and skills that must be addressed by elementary and secondary
teachers throughout the course of students' time at school.

Reader's Theatre or **Reader's theatre** is a style of theatre in which the
actors do not memorize their lines. Actors use only vocal expression
to help the audience understand the story rather than visual storytelling such as sets, costumes, intricate blocking, and movement.
This style of performance of literature was initially lauded because
it emphasized hearing a written text as a new way to understand
literature.

Reconciliation is a process of coming-together to restore or improve
the relations among parties that are formerly at odds with one another. In the treatment of moral and political issues, the concept of
reconciliation arises in the aftermath of wrongdoing and conflict
between persons and groups. The process of reconciliation must
involve acknowledging the wrongs of the past and the proper standing of victims (Bates et al., 2020). Although there has not been an
agreement of how precisely such acknowledgements are best communicated, common ways include formal apologies, memorials, truth
telling, and reparations.

Residential schools were government-funded, usually church-run,
boarding schools that were established to "assimilate Aboriginal
people forcibly into the Canadian mainstream by eliminating parental and community involvement in the intellectual, cultural, and
spiritual development of Aboriginal children" (Truth and Reconciliation Commission of Canada, 2015, p. 1). Amendments to the Indian

Act of 1876 in Canada provided for the creation of the Indian Residential School system. During that era, over 130 residential schools were located across the country, and the last school closed in 1996. More than 150,000 First Nations, Inuit, and Metis children were forcibly placed in these schools. They commonly were forbidden to speak their language or engage in their cultural and spiritual practices. There are an estimated 80,000 former students living today. The ongoing impact of the century-long school system has been felt throughout generations and has contributed to social problems that continue to exist. On June 11, 2008, the prime minister, on behalf of the Government of Canada, delivered a formal apology in the House of Commons to former students, their families, and communities for Canada's role in the operation of the residential schools.

Role drama, also known as process drama, is a form of theatre-making and improvisational drama work for the purpose of education. In role drama, performance for an external audience is absent. Students, along with their teacher, establish a sort of theatrical ensemble engaging in a series of improvisational activities as a way to understand and make meaning about issues or curricular concepts.

A **settler** is a person who migrated with a group of others to settle in a new region or colony. It is also used to describe people whose ancestors established a colony in the land that is traditional First Nation territory.

Tableau (Tableaux as plural) is one drama technique in which groups create a still image, especially on a stage, to represent a scene, an event, or a view of life.

Teacher in role is one drama strategy in which a teacher plays a role in the drama and collaborates with the students within the imaginary situation. The fictitious roles allow the teacher to help keep the drama in motion by questioning, challenging, organizing thoughts, and involving students. Through dramatic action, the teacher can engage students in using targeted language, point out consequences, and summarize ideas.

Truth and Reconciliation Commission of Canada (TRC) was officially launched in 2008 as part of the Indian Residential Schools Settlement Agreement (IRSSA). Intended to be a process that would guide Canadians through the difficult discovery of the facts behind the residential school system, the TRC was also meant to lay the foundation for lasting reconciliation across Canada (Moran, 2015). In general sense, a **truth commission** or **truth and reconciliation commission** is a commission tasked with discovering and revealing past wrongdoing usually by a government, in the hope of resolving conflict left over from the past. A collection of truth commissions around the world can be found in The Margarita S. Studemeister Digital Collections in International Conflict Management (https://www.usip.org/publications-tools/digital-collections).

A **vignette** is a short literary sketch to describe an event, happening, circumstance, or other episode.

References

Agamben, G. (2004). *The open: Man and animal* (K. Attell, Trans.). Stanford University Press.

Ahluwalia, S., Atkinson, S., Bishop, P., Christie, P., Hattam, R., & Matthews, J. (2012). *Reconciliation and pedagogy*. Routledge.

Amabile, T.M., & Pratt, M.G. (2016). The dynamic componential model of creativity and innovation in organizations: Making progress, making meaning. *Research in Organizational Behavior, 36*, 157–83. https://doi.org/10.1016/j.riob.2016.10.001

Appiah, A. (2018). *The lies that bind: Rethinking identity, creed, country, color, class, culture*. Liveright.

Apple, M. (1990). On analyzing hegemony. In M. Apple (Ed.), *Ideology and curriculum* (2nd ed., pp. 1–25). Routledge.

Apple, M., & Franklin, B. (1990). Curricular history and social control. In M. Apple (Ed.), *Ideology and curriculum* (2nd ed., pp. 61–81). Routledge.

Araya, D., & Peters, M. (2010). *Education in the creative economy: Knowledge and learning in the age of innovation*. Peter Lang.

Archibald, J. (2008). *Indigenous story work: Educating the heart, mind, body and spirit*. UBC Press.

Aristotle. (2013). *Physics* (C.D.C. Reeves, Trans.). Hackett. (Original work published ca. 350 B.C.E.)

Babayants, A., & Frey, H.F. (Eds.). (2015). *Theatre and learning*. Cambridge Scholars Publishing.

Ball, S.J. (2017). *The education debate*. Policy Press.

Ballard, R. & Ballard, S. (2011). From narrative inheritance to narrative momentum: Past, present, and future stories in an international adoptive family. *Journal of Family Communication 11*(2), 69–84, https://doi.org/10.1080/15267431.2011.554618

Bamford, A. (2009). *The wow factor: Global research compendium on the impact of the arts in education* (2nd ed.). Waxmann Verlag.

Bang, M., & Marin, A. (2015). Nature–culture constructs in science learning: Human/non-human agency and intentionality. *Journal of Research in Science Teaching, 52*(4), 530–44. https://doi.org/10.1002/tea.21204

Barad, K. (2014). Diffracting diffraction: Cutting together-apart. *Parallax, 20*(3), 168–87. https://doi.org/10.1080/13534645.2014.927623

Barker, H. (1997). *Arguments for a theatre* (3rd ed.). Manchester University Press.

Bates, G., Cinar, I., & Nalepa, M. (2020). Accountability by numbers: A new global transitional justice dataset (1946–2016). *Perspectives on Politics, 18*(1), 161–84. https://doi.org/10.1017/S1537592719000756

Beaucage, M. (2019, October 3). *Opening Speech.* More than Words event, McGill University Faculty Club.

Belliveau, G. (2015). Performing identity through research-based theatre: Brothers. *Journal of Educational Enquiry, 14*(1), 5–16.

Benedetti, R.L. (1976). *Seeming, being, and becoming: Acting in our century.* Drama Book Specialists.

Benedetti, R.L. (2008). *The actor at work.* Pearson.

Bishop, A. (2014). Non-indigenous ally. In D. Coghlan & M. Brydon-Miller (Eds.) *The SAGE Encyclopedia of Action Research.* SAGE Publications.

Black, J. (2014). *The REDress project.* Jaime Black. https://www.jaimeblackartist.com/exhibitions/

Blackstock, C. (2019, April 4). *How to change systemic racism in Canada* [Video]. YouTube. https://youtu.be/j-xAloD75dQ

Boal, A. (1979). *Theatre of the oppressed.* Theatre Communication Group.

Bochner, A.P., & Riggs, N.A. (2014). Practicing narrative inquiry. In P. Leavy (Ed.), *The Oxford handbook of qualitative research* (pp. 195–222). Oxford University Press.

Boghossian, P., & Lindsay, J. (2019). *How to have impossible conversations: A very practical guide.* Da Capo Lifelong Books.

Braidotti, R. (2013). *The posthuman.* Polity.

Braidotti, R. (2017). *Aspirations of a posthumanist.* [Video.] Youtube. https://www.youtube.com/watch?v=LNIYOKfRQks

Braidotti, R. (2019). A theoretical framework for the critical posthumanities. *Theory, Culture & Society, 36*(6), 31–61. https://doi.org/10.1177/0263276418771486

Bramwell, G., Reilly, R.C., Lilly, F.R., Kronish, N., & Chennabathni, R. (2011). Creative teachers. *Roeper Review, 33*(4), 228–38. https://doi.org/10.1080/02783193.2011.603111

Brant-Birioukov, K., Ng-A-Fook, N., & Kane, R. (2020). Reconceptualizing teacher education in Ontario: Civic particularity, ethical engagement, and reconciliation. In A. Phelan, W. Pinar, N. Ng-A-Fook, & R. Kane (Eds.),

Reconceptualizing teacher education: A Canadian contribution to a global challenge (pp. 39–66). University of Ottawa Press.

Bruner, J. (2002). Narrative distancing: A foundation of literacy. In J. Brockmeier, M. Wang, & D.R. Olson (Eds.), *Literacy, narrative and culture* (pp. 86–93). Curzon.

Butler-Kisber, L. (2002). Artful portrayals in qualitative inquiry: The road to found poetry and beyond. *The Alberta Journal of Educational Research, 48*(3), 229–39.

Butler-Kisber, L. (2010). *Qualitative inquiry: Thematic, narrative and arts-informed perspectives.* SAGE Publications.

Byrne, B. (2006). Moving horizons: Exploring the role of stories in decolonizing the literacy education of white teachers. *International Education, 37*(1), 114–31.

Cajete, G.A. (2006). Western science and the loss of natural creativity. In D.T. Jacobs (Ed.), *Unlearning the language of conquest: Scholars expose anti-Indianism in America* (pp. 247–59). University of Texas Press.

Canadian Press. (2019, July 23). *Opponents of Quebec religious symbols bill to appeal decision to maintain law.* Global News. https://globalnews.ca/news/5671303/opponents-of-quebec-religious-symbols-bill-to-appeal-decision-to-maintained-law/

Canadian Press. (2020, February 8). Quebec school board renounces federal funding for its Bill 21 court challenge. battlefordsNOW. https://battlefordsnow.com/2020/02/08/Québec-school-board-renounces-federal-funding-for-its-bill-21-court-challenge/

Cardin, J. (2004). Le nouveau programme d'histoire au secondaire: Le choix d'éduquer à lacitoyenneté. *Formation et profession: Bulletin du CRIFPE, 10*(2), 44–8.

Carpenter, P. (2019, May 6). Beaconsfield students learn about Indigenous history through the arts. *Global News.* https://globalnews.ca/news/5671303/opponents-of-Québec-religious-symbols-bill-to-appeal-decision-to-maintained-law/

Carr, P., & Klassen, T. (1997). Different perceptions of race in education: Racial minority and white teachers. *Canadian Journal of Education, 22*(1), 67–81. https://doi.org/10.2307/1585812

Carter, M. (2014). Drama and theatre education in Canada: A snapshot. *McGill Journal of Education, 49*(1), 237–45. https://doi.org/10.7202/1025780ar

Carter, M. (2014a). *The teacher monologues: Exploring the identities and experiences of artist-teachers.* Sense Publications.

Carter, M. (2014b). Imagination: Hope for a severed curriculum. In M.J. Harkins & Z. Barchuk (Eds.), *International conversations of teacher educators:*

Teaching and learning in a global world (pp. 80–94). Mount Saint Vincent University Press.

Carter, M. (2014c). Complicating the curricular conversation with Antonin Artaud and Maxine Greene. *Journal of the Canadian Association for Curriculum Studies, 11*(2), 21–43.

Carter, M.R. (2016). Postcards from prison: An auto-phenomenological inquiry. *JCT (Online), 31*(1), 72.

Carter, M., & Mreiwed, H. (2017). Sing the brave song: This isn't over. *Art/Research International, 2*(2), 153–7.

Carter, M., Prendergast, M., & Belliveau, G. (Eds.). (2015). *Drama and theatre education in Canada: Classroom and community contexts.* Canadian Association for Teacher Education/Canadian Society for the Study of Education.

Carter, M., Wiebe, S., Gouzouasis, P., Shuman, L., McLarnon, M., Ricketts, K., Howard, P., & Fischer, B. (2020). Reconceptualizing teacher identity through design thinking: A Montreal case study. *Canadian Art Teacher, 17*(1), 24–37.

Carvel, J. (2000, January 3). Constant criticism unsets teachers. *The Guardian.* https://www.theguardian.com/education/2000/jan/03/teaching.schools

Catterall, J.S. (2002). The arts and the transfer of learning. In R. Deasy (Ed.), *Critical links: Learning in the arts and student academic and social development.* Arts Education Partnership.

CBC News. (2017, March 29). *Senator Murray Sinclair responds to Lynn Beyak's residential school remarks* [Video]. Youtube. https://www.youtube.com/watch?v=BVjHGNreBkU

Cerbone, D. (2006). *Understanding phenomenology.* Acumen.

Charlton, J.I. (2000). *Nothing about us without us: Disability oppression and empowerment.* University of California Press.

Clandinin, D.J., & Connelly, F.M. (2000). *Narrative inquiry: Experience and story in qualitative research.* Jossey-Bass.

Clarkson, A. (2014). *Belonging: The paradox of citizenship.* House of Anansi Press.

Clément, V. (2016). Dancing bodies and indigenous ontology: What does the haka reveal about the Māori relationship with the earth? *Transactions of the Institute of British Geographers, 42*(2), 317–28. https://doi.org/10.1111/tran.12157

Cochran-Smith, M. (2000). Blind-vision: Unlearning racism in teacher education. *Harvard Educational Review, 70,* 157–90. https://doi.org/10.17763/haer.70.2.e77x215054558564

Cohen, L. (1992). Anthem [Song]. On *The Future.* Columbia.

Coleman, E. (2005). *Aboriginal art, identity, and appropriation.* Ashgate Publishing.

Connerton, P. (1989). *How Societies Remember.* Cambridge University Press. https://doi.org/10.1017/CBO9780511628061

Coole, D., & Frost, S. (2010). *New materialisms.* Duke University Press.

Courtney, R. (1986). Drama as a generic skill. *Youth Theatre Journal*, *1*(1), 10–27.

Craft, A. (2002). *Creativity and early years education: A lifewide foundation.* Continuum International Publishing Group.

Crenshaw, K. (1991). Mapping the margins: Intersectionality, identity politics, and violence against women of color. *Stanford Law Review, 43*(6), 1241–99. https://doi.org/10.2307/1229039

Creswell, J.W. (2014). *Educational research: Planning, conducting and evaluating quantitative and qualitative research* (4th ed.). Pearson.

Cropley, A.J. (1999). Creativity and cognition: Producing effective novelty. *Roeper Review: A Journal on Gifted Education, 21*(4), 253–60. https://doi.org/10.1080/02783199909553972

Crown-Indigenous Relations and Northern Affairs Canada. (2018, December 6). *Agreement-in-principle reached to resolve Indian Day Schools litigation.* [Press release]. https://www.canada.ca/en/crown-indigenous-relations-northern-affairs/news/2018/12/agreement-in-principle-reached-to-resolve-indian-day-schools-litigation.html

de Britto, F. (2018). Neither hired mouth nor class monarchs: The scope of schoolteachers' freedom of expression in Canada. *Canadian Journal of Education, 41*(3), 783–807. https://www.jstor.org/stable/e26570559

Deleuze, G., & Guattari, F. (1987). *A thousand plateaus: Capitalism and schizophrenia.* University of Minnesota Press.

Derrida, J. (2002). *On cosmopolitanism and forgiveness.* Routledge.

Dewey, J. (1934). *Art as experience.* Penguin Books.

Dewey, J. (1998). *Experience and education: The 60th anniversary.* Kappa Delta Pi.

Diversi, M., & Moreira, C. (2009). *Betweener talk: Decolonizing knowledge production, pedagogy, and praxis.* University of Chicago Press.

Donald, D. (2012). Forts, colonial frontier logics, and Aboriginal-Canadian relations: Imagining decolonizing educational philosophies in Canadian contexts. In A.A. Abdi (Ed.), *Decolonizing philosophies of education* (pp. 91–111). Sense Publishers.

Donmoyer, R., & Yennie-Donmoyer, J. (2008). Readers' theater as a data display strategy. In J.G. Coles & A.L. Knowles (Eds.), *Handbook of the arts in qualitative research* (pp. 209–24). SAGE Publications.

Droznin, A. (2016). *Physical actor training: What shall I do with the body they gave me?* Taylor & Francis.

Dubuc, B. (2002). *The brain from top to bottom.* https://thebrain.mcgill.ca

Eddo-Lodge, R. (2017). *Why I'm no longer talking to white people about race.* Bloomsbury Publishing.

Edwards, A. (2015). Recognising and realising teachers' professional agency. *Teachers and Teaching, 21*(6), 779–84. https://doi.org/10.1080/13540602.2015.1044333

Eisner, E. (1979). *The educational imagination.* Macmillan Publishers.

Eisner, E.W. (2002). *The arts and the creation of mind.* Yale University Press.

Ellis, C., & Flaherty, M. (1992). *Investigating subjectivity: Research on lived experience* (Vol. 139). SAGE Publications.

Erikson, E.H. (1959). *Identity and the life cycle: Selected papers.* International Universities Press.

Erikson, E.H. (1968). *Identity: Youth and crisis* (No. 7). W. W. Norton & Company.

Erikson, E.H. (1979). *Dimensions of a new identity.* W. W. Norton & Company.

Erikson, E.H. (1993). *Childhood and society.* W. W. Norton & Company. (Original work published 1950)

Escobar, A. (2007). The 'ontological turn' in social theory. A commentary on 'Human geography without scale,' by Sallie Marston, John Paul Jones II and Keith Woodward. *Transactions of the Institute of British Geographer, 32*(1), 106–11.

Esteban-Guitart, M. (2014). Appropriation. In T. Teo (Ed.), *Encyclopedia of critical psychology.* Springer.

Felman, S. (1982). Psychoanalysis and education: Teaching terminable and interminable. *Yale French Studies, 63*, 21–44. https://doi.org/10.2307 /2929829

Fels, L. (1999). *In the wind clothes dance on a clothes line: Performative inquiry – a(re) search methodology* [Unpublished doctoral dissertation]. University of British Columbia.

Fenske, M. (2004). The aesthetic of the unfinished: Ethics and performance. *Performance Quarterly, 24*(1), 1–19. https://doi.org/10.1080 /1046293042000239447

Fischer, B. (2019). *Sustaining creativity: How postsecondary teachers reinvest in innovative practices over the course of a career* [Unpublished doctoral dissertation]. McGill University.

Fischer, B., & Golden, J. (2018). Modelling and fostering creativity: Two post-secondary EAL teachers' journey. *Canadian Journal of Education/Revue Canadienne De l'éducation, 41*(1), 98–123. Retrieved from https://journals .sfu.ca/cje/index.php/cje-rce/article/view/2474

Fiske, E. (Ed.). (1999). *Champions of change: The impact of arts on learning.* The Arts Education Partnership and the President's Committee on the Arts and Humanities.

Fitzpatrick, E. (2018). A Story of Becoming: Entanglement, Settler Ghosts, and Postcolonial Counterstories. *Cultural Studies ↔ Critical Methodologies, 18*(1), 43– 51. https://doi.org/10.1177/1532708617728954

Fontaine, P., & Craft, A. (2015). *A knock on the door: The essential history of residential schools from the Truth and Reconciliation Commission of Canada.* University of Manitoba Press.

Foucault, M. (1977). *Language, counter-memory, practice: Selected essays and interviews by Michel Foucault.* Cornell Publications.

Foucault, M. (1980). *Power/knowledge: Selected interviews and other writings, 1972–1977.* Vintage.

Foucault, M. (1984). *The Foucault reader.* Pantheon Books.

Freedman, P., & Holmes, M. (2003). *The teacher's body: Embodiment, authority, and identity in the academy.* State University of New York Press.

Freire, P. (1968). *Pedagogy of the oppressed.* Verlag Herder.

Funk, A. (2019). Curriculum and creativity [Unpublished doctoral paper]. Department of Integrated Studies in Education, McGill University.

Gadamer, H.G. (1997). 15 Rhetoric, hermeneutics, and ideology-critique. In W. Jost & M.J. Hyde (Eds.), *Rhetoric and hermeneutics in our time* (pp. 313–34). Yale University Press.

Gadamer, H.G. (2003). *Forstaelsens filosofi.* Cappelen.

Gallagher, S. (2000). Philosophical conceptions of the self: Implications for cognitive science. *Trends in cognitive sciences, 4*(1), 14–21. https://doi.org/10.1016/S1364-6613(99)01417-5

Gallagher, K. (2000). *Drama education in the lives of girls.* University of Toronto Press.

Gallagher, K., & Booth, D. (2003). *How theatre educates: Convergences and counterpoints with artists, scholars and advocates.* University of Toronto Press.

Ginsberg, A.E. (2012). *Embracing risk in urban education: Curiosity, creativity, and courage in the era of "no excuses" and relay race reform.* Rowman & Littlefield.

George, D. (1970). Preface. In G. Ryga & C. Crowell (Eds.), *The ecstasy of Rita Joe* (p. 1). Talonbooks.

Giroux, H.A., & Penna, A.N. (1979). Social education in the classroom: The dynamics of the hidden curriculum. *Theory & Research in Social Education, 7*(1), 21–42. https://doi.org/10.1080/00933104.1979.10506048

Goodson, I. (1989). Curriculum reform and curriculum theory: A case of historical amnesia. *Cambridge Journal of Education, 19*(2), 131–41. https://doi.org/10.1080/0305764890190203

Greene, M. (1995). *Releasing the imagination: Essays on education, the arts, and social change.* Jossey-Bass.

Greene, M. (2012). Foreword. In A.E. Ginsberg (Ed.), *Embracing risk in urban education: Curiosity, creativity, and courage in the era of "no excuses" and relay race reform* (pp. vii–viii). Rowman & Littlefield.

Grumet, M. (1988). *Bitter milk.* University of Massachusetts Press.

Hare, J. (2020). Reconciliation in teacher education: Hope or hype? In A. Phelan, W. Pinar, N. Ng-A-Fook. & R. Kane (Eds.), *Reconceptualizing teacher education: A Canadian contribution to a global challenge* (pp. 39–66). University of Ottawa Press.

Hare, J. (2011). Learning from Indigenous knowledge in education. In Long & Dickason (Eds.), *Visions of the heart.* Oxford University Press.

Halberstam, J. (2011). *The queer art of failure*. Duke University Press.

Hallam, B. (2011, February 7). Author generating critical hope in approach to reconciliation. *UVic News*. https://www.uvic.ca/news/topics /2011+paulette-regan+ring

Hammer, K. (1992). John O'Neal, actor and activist: The praxis of storytelling. In A. Bean (Ed.), *A sourcebook on African-American performance: Plays, people, movement*. Routledge.

Harris, A. (2014). *The creative turn: Toward a new aesthetic imaginary*. Sense Publishers.

Hattam, R. (2020). From South African black theology and Freire to 'teaching for resistance': The work of Basil Moore. In S.R. Steinberg & B. Down (Eds.), *The SAGE handbook of critical pedagogies*. SAGE Publications.

Heidegger, M. (1962). *Being and time* (J. Macquarrie & E. Robinson, Trans.). Harper. (Original work published 1927)

Henry, E., & Pene, H. (2001). Kaupapa Maori: locating Indigenous ontology, epistemology and methodology. *Organization, 8*(2), 234–42. https://doi.org /10.1177%2F1350508401082009

Higgins, M., & Maddens, B. (2019). Refiguring presences in Kichwa-Lamista territories: Natural, cultural, (re)storying with Indigenous place. In C. Taylor & A. Bayley (Eds.), *Posthumanism and higher education*. Palgrave Macmillan.

Howard, P. (2018, June 11). The problem with blackface. *The Conversation*. https://theconversation.com/the-problem-with-blackface-97987

Huebner, D.E., Pinar, W., & Hillis, V. (1999). *The lure of the transcendent: Collected essays*. Lawrence Erlbaum Associates.

Hughes, P.M. (2011). Political forgiveness. In D.K. Chatterjee (Ed.), *Encyclopedia of global justice*. Springer.

Husserl, E. (1965). *Phenomenology and the crisis of philosophy: Philosophy as a rigorous science, and philosophy and the crisis of European man*. Harper & Row.

Isaksen, S.G., & Akkermans, H.J. (2011). Creative climate: A leadership lever for innovation. *Journal of Creative Behavior, 45*(3), 161–87. https://doi. org/10.1002/j.2162-6057.2011.tb01425.x

Indigenous Tourism Association of Canada. (n.d.). *Indigenous Canada*. https://indigenoustourism.ca/en/

Jones, A., & Jenkins, K. (2008). Rethinking collaboration: Working the indigene-colonizer hyphen. In N. Denzin, Y. Lincoln, & L. Tuhiwai Smith (Eds.), *Handbook of critical and Indigenous methodologies* (pp. 471–86). SAGE Publications.

Joseph, R.P. (2018). *21 things you may not know about the Indian Act*. Indigenous Relations Press.

Justice, D.H. (2018). *Why Indigenous literatures matter*. Wilfrid Laurier University Press.

KAIROS Blanket Exercise Community. (n.d.). Reconciliation through education and understanding. Retrieved 22 March 2020, from https://www.kairosblanketexercise.org

Kant, I. (1965). The doctrine of virtue (M.J. Gregor, Trans.). *Ethics, 75*(2), 142–43.

Kerr, J. (2019). Indigenous education in higher education in Canada. In C. Taylor & A. Bayley (Eds.), *Posthumanism and higher education*. Palgrave Macmillan.

Kerr, J., & Andreotti, V. (2019). Crossing borders in initial teacher education: Mapping dispositions to diversity and inequity. *Race Ethnicity and Education, 22*(5), 647–65. https://doi.org/10.1080/13613324.2017.1395326

Kolodziechuk, A. (2017). Sing the brave song. Unpublished play.

Kumar, A. (2013). *Curriculum as meditative inquiry*. Palgrave Macmillan.

LaDuke, W. (2017). *All our relations: Native struggles for land and life*. Haymarket Books.

Large, W. (2008). *Heidegger's being and time*. Indiana University Press.

Leavitt, S. (2020, February 8). Quebec passes education reforms abolishing school boards. *CBC News*. https://www.cbc.ca/news/canada/montreal/quebec-education-reform-school-boards-1.5457100

Leavy, P. (2009). *Method meets art: Arts-based research practice*. Guilford Press.

Lecun, Y., & Hollister, M. (2017, October 17). *Disruption in the workplace: Artificial intelligence in the 21st Century* [Video]. Youtube. https://www.youtube.com/watch?v=OgW4e_ZY26s

Leggo, C. (2008). Narrative inquiry: Attending to the art of discourse. *Language and Literacy, 10*(1), 1–21. https://doi.org/10.20360/G2SG6Q

Lévesque, S. (2004). History and social studies in Quebec: An historical perspective. In A. Sear, & I. Wright (Eds.), *Challenges and prospects for Canadian social studies* (pp. 55–72). Pacific Educational Press.

Lewis, T., & Kahn, R. (2010). *Education out of bounds: Reimagining cultural studies for the posthuman age*. Palgrave Macmillan.

Lewis, T.E., & Owen, J. (2020). Posthuman phenomenologies: Performance philosophy, non-human animals, and the landscape. *Qualitative Inquiry, 26*(5), 472–78.

Long, D. & Dickason, P. (2011). *Visions of the heart*. Oxford University Press.

Lyotard, J. (1991). *The inhuman: Reflections on time*. Polity Press, Cambridge.

Mackey, E. (2002). *The house of difference: Cultural politics and national identity in Canada*. University of Toronto Press.

Madden, B. (2019). A de/colonizing theory of truth and reconciliation education. *Curriculum Inquiry, 49*(3), 284–312. https://doi.org/10.1080/03626784.2019.1624478

Magrini, J. (2014). *Social efficiency and instrumentalism in education*. Routledge.

Mama, A. (1995). Feminism or femocracy? State feminism and democratisation in Nigeria. *Africa Development/Afrique et Développement, 20*(1), 37–58. https://www.jstor.org/stable/43657968

Massumi, B. (2015). *Politics of affect.* John Wiley & Sons.

Maxwell, J.A., & Miller, B. (2008). Categorizing and connecting strategies in qualitative data analysis. In S.N. Hesse-Biber & P. Leavy (Eds.), *Handbook of emergent methods* (pp. 461–77). Guilford Press.

Maykut, P. & Morehouse, R. (1994). *Beginning qualitative research: A philosophic and practical guide.* Routledge Falmer Publisher.

McKinnon, J., & Upton, R. (2015). Using learning centered method to address the pedagogical and creative challenges of the classroom production. In A. Babayants & H.F. Frey (Eds.), *Theatre and learning* (pp. 115–37). Cambridge Scholars Publishing.

McNay, M. (2009). Absent memory, family secrets, narrative inheritance. *Qualitative Inquiry (15)*7, 1178–88. https://doi.org/10.1177/1077800409334236

Merleau-Ponty, M. (1964). *The primacy of perception and other essays on phenomenological psychology, the philosophy of art, history and politics.* Northwestern University Press.

Merleau-Ponty, M. (1996). *Phenomenology of perception.* Motilal Banarsidass Publisher.

Merriam-Webster Dictionary. (n.d.). Risk. In *Merriam-Webster.com dictionary.* Retrieved 14 December 2019, from https://www.merriam-webster.com/dictionary/risk

Merriam-Webster Dictionary. (n.d.a). Danger. In *Merriam-Webster.com dictionary.* Retrieved 19 January 2019, from https://www.merriam-webster.com/dictionary/danger

Merriam, S.B. (1998). *Qualitative research and case study applications in education. Revised and expanded from "Case Study Research in Education."* Jossey-Bass Publishers.

Mienczakowski, J. (1995). The theater of ethnography: The reconstruction of ethnography into theater with emancipatory potential. *Qualitative Inquiry 1*(3), 360–75. https://doi.org/10.1177/107780049500100306

Mika, C.T.H. (2015). The thing's revelation: Some thoughts on Māori philosophical research. *Waikato Journal of Education, 20*(2), 61–8.

Miller, J.R. (1999). Residential schools in Canada. In J.H. Marsh (Ed.), *The Canadian encyclopedia* (p. 1582). Historica Canada.

Ministère de l'Éducation et de l'Enseignement supérieur [MEES]. (2016). *Quebec Education Plan.* Gouvernment du Québec. http://eee.education.gouv.qc.ca/en/teachers/quebec-education-program

Ministère de l'Éducation et de l'Enseignement supérieur [MEES]. (2001). *Arts education.* http://www.education.gouv.qc.ca/fileadmin/site_web/documents/education/jeunes/pfeq/PFEQ_art-dramatique-primaire_EN.pdf

Ministère de l'Éducation et de l'Enseignement supérieur [MEES]. (n.d.). *Legislation.* http://www.education.gouv.qc.ca/en/contenus-communs /parents-and-guardians/instruction-in-english/legislation

Ministère de l'Éducation. (1998). *A school for the future: Policy statement on educational integration and intercultural education.* Gouvernment du Québec. http://www.education.gouv.qc.ca/fileadmin/site_web/documents/dpse /adaptation_serv_compl/PolitiqueMatiereIntegrationScolEduc Interculturelle_UneEcoleAvenir_a.pdf

Ministère de l'Éducation, du Loisir et du Sport [MELS]. (2003). *Programme de formation de l'école québécoise.* http://www.education.gouv.qc.ca/fileadmin /site_web/documents/education/jeunes/pfeq/PFEQ-tableau-synthese -secondaire-cycles-1-et-2.pdf

Moran, R. (2015, September 24). *Truth and Reconciliation Commission.* The Canadian Encyclopedia. https://www.thecanadianencyclopedia.ca/en /article/truth-and-reconciliation-commission

Moustakas, C. (1994). *Phenomenological research methods.* SAGE Publications.

Mreiwed, H., Carter, M.R., & Shabtay, A. (2017). Building classroom community through drama education. *NJ: Drama Australia Journal, 41*(1), 44–57. https://doi.org/10.1080/14452294.2017.1329680

Nancy, J. (2000). *Being singular plural.* Stanford University Press.

Norris, J. (2000). Drama as research: Realizing the potential of drama in education as a research methodology. *Youth Theatre International, 14*(3), 40–51. https://doi.org/10.1080/08929092.2000.10012516

O'Connor, F., Fitzgerald, S., & Fitzgerald, R. (1969). *Mystery and manners: Occasional prose.* Farrar, Straus & Giroux.

Oluo, I. (2019). *So you want to talk about race.* Hachette.

Palmer, P. (2007). *The courage to teach.* John Wiley & Sons.

Parrott, Z. (2007). Indigenous people in Canada. *The Canadian encyclopedia.* https://www.thecanadianencyclopedia.ca/en/article/aboriginal-people

Patterson, J. (1994). Maori environmental virtues. *Environmental Ethics, 16,* 397–409.

Perry, M. (2015). Reconsidering good intentions: Learning with failure in education and the arts. In A. Babayants & H.F. Frey (Eds.), *Theatre and learning* (pp. 138–52). Cambridge Scholars Publishing.

Phelan, A.M., & Rüsselbæk Hansen, D. (2018). Reclaiming agency and appreciating limits in teacher education: Existential, ethical and psychoanalytical readings. *McGill Journal of Education, 53*(1), 128–45.

Phelan, A., Pinar, W., Ng-A-Fook, N., & Kane, R. (Eds). (2020). *Reconceptualizing teacher education: A Canadian contribution to a global challenge.* University of Ottawa Press.

Pinar, W.F. (1975). Currere: Toward reconceptualization. In W. Pinar (Ed.), *Curriculum theorizing: The reconceptualists* (pp. 396–414). McCutchan Publishing.

Pinar, W.F., Reynolds, W.M., Slattery, P., & Taubman, P.M. (1995). *Understanding curriculum: An introduction to the study of historical and contemporary curriculum discourses.* Peter Lang.

Polkinghorne, D.E. (1995). Narrative configuration in qualitative analysis. In J.A. Hatch & R. Wisniewski (Eds.), *Life history and narrative* (pp. 5–23). Falmer Press.

Prentki, T., & Stinson, M. (2016). Relational pedagogy and the drama curriculum. *Research in Drama Education: The Journal of Applied Theatre and Performance, 21*(1), 1–12. https://doi.org/10.1080/13569783.2015.1127153

Regan, P. (2010). *Unsettling the settler within: Indian residential schools, truth telling, and reconciliation in Canada.* UBC Press.

Reilly, R.C., Lilly, F., Bramwell, G., & Kronish, N. (2011). A synthesis of research concerning creative teachers in a Canadian context. *Teaching and Teacher Education, 27*(3), 533–42. https://doi.org/10.1016/j.tate.2010.10.007

Roberts, M., Haami, B., Benton, R., Satterfield, T., Finucane, M., Henare, M., & Henare, M. (2004). Whakapapa as Maori mental construct: Some implications for the debate over genetic modification of organisms. *The Contemporary Pacific, 16*(1), 1–28. https://www.jstor.org/stable/23722949

Roman, L. (1993). On the ground with antiracist pedagogy and Raymond Williams's unfinished project to articulate a socially transformative critical Realism. In D. Dworkin & L. Roman (Eds.), *Views beyond the border country: Raymond Williams and cultural politics* (pp. 158–216). Routledge.

Rosenberg, P. (1997). Underground discourses: Exploring whiteness in teacher education. In M.E. Fine, L.E. Weis, L.C. Powell, & L. Wong (Eds.), *Off white: Readings on race, power and society* (pp. 79–89). Routledge.

Ryan, J., Pollock, K., & Antonelli, F. (2009). Teacher diversity in Canada: Leaky pipelines, bottlenecks and glass ceilings. *Canadian Journal of Education, 32*(3), 591–617. https://www.jstor.org/stable/canajeducrevucan.32.3.591

Ryga, G. (1970). *The ecstasy of Rita Joe.* Talonbooks.

Saad, G. (2020). *The parasitic mind: How infectious ideas are killing common sense.* Simon and Schuster.

Saldana, J. (2008). Ethnodrama and ethnotheatre. In J.G. Coles & A.L. Knowles (Eds.), *Handbook of the arts in qualitative research* (pp. 195–207). SAGE Publications.

Salehi, S. (2008). *Teaching contingencies: Deleuze, creativity discourses, and art* [Unpublished doctoral dissertation]. Queen's University.

Sartre, J.P. (1992). *Notebooks for an ethics.* University of Chicago Press.

Saunders, J.N. (2021). The power of the arts in learning and the curriculum: A review of research literature. *Curriculum Perspectives, 41*(1), 93–100.

Sawyer, R.K. (2006). *Explaining creativity: The science of human innovation.* Oxford University Press.

Schonmann, S. (Ed.). (2011). *Key concepts in theatre/drama education*. Springer Science & Business Media.

Sensoy, O., & DiAngelo, R. (2011). *Is everyone really equal?* Teacher's College Press.

Shabtay, A., Carter, M.R., & Mreiwed, H. (2019). A dramatic collage: Becoming pedagogical through collaborative playbuilding. *Qualitative Research Journal* 19(4), 403–414. https://doi.org/10.1108/QRJ-02-2019-0020

Sleeter, C., & Grant, C. (1987). An analysis of multicultural education in the United States. *Harvard Educational Review, 57*(4), 421–44.

Smith, L. (1999). *Decolonizing methodologies: Research and Indigenous peoples*. Zed Books.

Smith, S., & Watson, J. (Eds.). (1992). *De/Colonizing the subject: The politics of gender in women's autobiography*. University of Minnesota Press.

Smith, A.R., Chein, J., & Steinberg, L. (2013). Impact of socio-emotional context, brain development, and pubertal maturation on adolescent risk-taking. *Hormones and behavior, 64*(2), 323–32. https://doi.org/10.1016/j.yhbeh.2013.03.006

Snaza, N., Appelbaum, P., Bayne, S., Carlson, D., Morris, M., Rotas, N., Sandlin, J., Wallin, J., & Weaver, J. (2014). Toward a posthuman education. *Journal of Curriculum Theorizing, 30*(2), 39–55. https://digitalcommons.georgiasouthern.edu/curriculum-facpubs/47

St. Denis, V. (2011). Silencing Aboriginal curricular content and perspectives through multiculturalism: "There are other children here." *Review of Education, Pedagogy, and Cultural Studies, 33*(4), 306–17. https://doi.org/10.1080/10714413.2011.597638

Stanislavski, K.S. (1989). *An actor prepares* (E.R. Hapgood, Trans.). Routledge. (Original work published 1936)

Starblanket, T. (2019, December 14). *Is reconciliation a peaceful process?* Canadian Dimension. https://canadiandimension.com/articles/view/is-reconciliation-a-peaceful-process

Strauss, A., & Corbin, J. (1990). *Basics of qualitative research: Grounded theory procedures and techniques*. SAGE Publications.

Strong-Wilson, T. (2006). Re-visioning one's narratives: Exploring the relationship between researcher self-study and teacher research. *Studying Teacher Education, 2*(1), 59–76. https://doi.org/10.1080/17425960600557470

Strong-Wilson, T. (2007). Moving horizons: Exploring the role of stories in decolonizing the literacy education of white teachers. *International Education, 37*(1), 114–31.

Sumara, D., & Davis, B. (2006). *Complexity and education: Inquiries into learning, teaching, and research*. Lawrence Erlbaum Associates.

Sundberg, J. (2013). Decolonizing posthumanist geographies. *cultural geographies, 21*(1), 33–47.

Talaga, T. (2018). *All our relations.* House of Anansi Press.

Todd, Z. (2016). An Indigenous feminist's take on the ontological turn: 'Ontology' is just another word for colonialism. *Journal of Historical Sociology, 29*(1), 4–22. https://doi.org/10.1111/johs.12124

Truth and Reconciliation Commission of Canada (TRC). (2015). *Truth and Reconciliation Commission of Canada: Calls to action.* https://www.trc.ca/assets/pdf/Calls_to_Action_English2.pdf

Tuck, E., & Yang, K. (2012). Decolonization is not a metaphor. *Decolonization, Indigeneity, Education & Society, 1*(1), 1–40.

Van Manen, M. (1990). Beyond assumptions: Shifting the limits of action research. *Theory into practice, 29*(3), 152–57. https://doi.org/10.1080/00405849009543448

Wagamese, R. (2019). *One drum: Stories and ceremonies for a planet.* Douglas and McIntyre.

Wager, A. (2015). Hidden pedagogies at play: Street youth resisting within applied theatre. In A. Babayants, & H.F. Frey (Eds.), *Theatre and learning* (pp. 97–114). Cambridge Scholars Publishing.

Wales, P. (2009). Positioning the drama teacher: Exploring the power of identity in teaching practices. *RiDE: The Journal of Applied Theatre and Performance, 14*(2), 261–78. https://doi.org/10.1080/13569780902868911

Watters, H. (2015, June 1). *Truth and Reconciliation chair urges Canada to adopt UN declaration on Indigenous Peoples* [Video]. CBC News. https://www.cbc.ca/news/politics/truth-and-reconciliation-chair-urges-canada-to-adopt-un-declaration-on-indigenous-peoples-1.3096225

Weigler, W. (2001). *Strategies for playbuilding: Helping groups translate issues into theatre.* Heinemann Drama.

Wenger, E. (2000). *Communities of practice: Learning, meaning, identity.* Cambridge University Press.

Worth, P.J. (2000). *Localised creativity: A life span perspective* [Unpublished doctoral dissertation]. The Open University.

Worth, P.J. (2010). *Four questions of creativity: Keys to a creative life.* Trafford Publishing.

Yin, R. (1994). *Case study research: Design and methods.* SAGE Publications.

Young, B. (2006). Teaching about racism and anti-semitism in the context of Quebec's history programs. *Canadian Issues/Thèmes canadiens* (Fall), 91–6.

Young, J.O. (2010). *Cultural appropriation and the arts.* John Wiley & Sons.

Younging, G. (2018). *Elements of Indigenous style: A guide for writing by and about Indigenous peoples.* Brush Education.

Zanazanian, P. (2008). Historical consciousness and the "French-English" divide among Quebec history teachers. *Canadian Ethnic Studies/Études ethniques au Canada, 40*(3), 109–30. https://doi.org/10.1353/ces.2008.0013

Index

Page numbers in italics refer to figures; page number in bold refer to tables.

.

Printed and bound by CPI Group (UK) Ltd, Croydon, CR0 4YY

10/06/2025

14686726-0001